Mohamed Ac

A Framework and Methodology for Managing Quality
of Web Services

Mohamed Adel Serhani

A Framework and Methodology for Managing Quality of Web Services

Extending Service Oriented Architecture: SOA to support Web Service Management, QoWS Management and Web Service Composition Management

VDM Verlag Dr. Müller

Imprint

Bibliographic information by the German National Library: The German National Library lists this publication at the German National Bibliography; detailed bibliographic information is available on the Internet at http://dnb.d-nb.de.

Any brand names and product names mentioned in this book are subject to trademark, brand or patent protection and are trademarks or registered trademarks of their respective holders. The use of brand names, product names, common names, trade names, product descriptions etc. even without a particular marking in this works is in no way to be construed to mean that such names may be regarded as unrestricted in respect of trademark and brand protection legislation and could thus be used by anyone.

Cover image: www.purestockx.com

Publisher:
VDM Verlag Dr. Müller Aktiengesellschaft & Co. KG , Dudweiler Landstr. 125 a, 66123 Saarbrücken, Germany,
Phone +49 681 9100-698, Fax +49 681 9100-988,
Email: info@vdm-verlag.de

Zugl.: Montreal, Concordia, ECE, Diss., 2006.

Produced in USA and UK by:
Lightning Source Inc., La Vergne, Tennessee, USA
Lightning Source UK Ltd., Milton Keynes, UK
BookSurge LLC, 5341 Dorchester Road, Suite 16, North Charleston, SC 29418, USA

ISBN: 978-3-8364-5767-5

Abstract

A Framework and Methodology for Managing Quality of Web Services

Mohamed Adel Serhani, Ph.D.
Concordia University, 2006

The wide acceptance and adoption of the eXtensible Markup Language (XML) and related technologies led to the rise of a new paradigm for applications development. Web Services, largely based on XML and Internet protocols, extend the traditional role of the World Wide Web for a stronger support for business-to-business interactions.

The Web Services paradigm is based on the exposure of applications' functionality through XML-based interface descriptions which have the potential of making services available for various kinds of end-users including software programs. Another very promising future of Web services consists of the potential of composing basic Web services to produce more complex Web services with a wide range of functionalities. The Web services approach presents fundamental changes in the way systems are designed, developed, deployed and managed. The Service Oriented Architecture (SOA) was proposed to position the key players in this new paradigm where main operations will be executed using technologies such as SOAP, WSDL, and UDDI.

The rapidly emerging efforts to automate the use of Web services are a great indicator that Web services are becoming a key future strategic direction of research for academia and industry. The management of quality of Web services (QoWS), as integral part of Web services management will play an important role for the success of this emerging technology and its adoption by services providers and consumers.

In this thesis, we investigate the management of QoWS for basic and composite Web services by taking it into consideration as part of a systematic process for the development of Web services. We studied the development of a new framework that intends to capture major management operations and the necessary extensions of SOA to support QoWS management. The proposed framework is divided into three layers: (1) QoWS design methodology and patterns layer, (2) QoWS management for basic Web service layer and (3) QoWS management for composite Web service layer. The first layer provides mechanisms that include design principals and methodology for QoWS specification, management, negotiation, and composition. The second layer provides operations of QoWS management for basic Web services. The third layer extends the work for QoWS management operations for composite Web services.

Table of Contents

List of Figures

List of Tables

Chapter 1

Introduction

1.1 Research Area

The new development of Internet technologies, largely affected by the eXtensible Markup Language (XML) and related technologies, is extending the traditional role (client-to-business) of the World Wide Web for a better support for business-to-business interactions. The future perspective of the Internet is being driven by a new concept most known as Web services.

A Web Service can be defined as an application that exposes its functionality through an interface description and makes it available for use by other programs. A composite Web service can further be created by aggregating a set of Web services to produce a more complex Web service with a wide range of functionalities. Web services allow computers and devices to interact with each other using the Internet to exchange and gather data in new ways. The importance of Web services has been recognized and widely accepted by industry and academic researchers. Academics have been mostly concerned with the expressiveness of service description, while industry has focused on Web services languages, protocols and architectures. The rapidly emerging efforts to automate the use of Web services are a great indicator that Web services are becoming a key future research direction.

Management of Web services as well as their quality of service is expected to become more and more important as the number of Web services available on the Internet proliferates and the need for composite Web services increases.

The management of quality of Web services (QoWS), as integral part of the Web service management will play an important role for the success of this emerging technology. On one hand, providers of Web services will need to specify and guarantee QoWS to remain competitive and achieve the highest possible revenue from their business. On the other hand, clients will have the possibility to look for good services (e.g. high availability, short response time, etc.).

Provision of acceptable QoWS is a challenging task due to the dynamic and unpredictable nature of the Web. In contrast to QoS management in centralized systems, QoWS management in distributed systems depends on its environment composition (Network performance, Servers, Database access, etc.). Therefore QoWS management will be a critical and significant challenge because of the dynamic and unpredictable nature of business applications and Internet traffic.

The work presented in this thesis is concerned with QoWS management for basic and composite Web services. The focus is first on building a systematic way of developing Web services taking into consideration QoWS management. As part of QoWS management, we introduced some ideas for the management of QoS of composite Web services. Along with this thesis, we propose solutions for QoS management of basic and composite Web services.

Web services are sometime referred to in the literature using different terms. Some authors use the term 'XML Web Services', other use Web Services and capitalize the beginning letters 'W' and 'S', also some other authors use 'service' is singular instead of 'services'. We will use the term "Web services" along in this thesis. The term QoS is often used in the context of networking, multimedia applications and telephony which may not represent the same meaning in the context of Web services. We will use the term Quality of Web services (QoWS) to emphasize the QoS context of this research.

The remaining chapter presents the problem statement, objectives and contributions, and finally the structure and the organization of the thesis.

1.2 Problem Statement

Web services are increasingly used as a new technology for providing and/or consuming services artifacts via the Internet. The Web services approach presents fundamental changes in the way systems are designed, developed, deployed and managed. At the earlier stages of the emergence of Web services as new paradigm, the focus was on the definition of protocols, standards, development environments and interfaces. As the Web services concepts and related standards become more mature; the need for a reformulation and standardization of a development process of Web services become very urgent. New development lifecycle for Web services is supposed to integrate features such as QoWS-driven Web services selection, QoWS management, and QoWS composition enforcement and management. These features (patterns) need to be addressed in earlier phases through Web services development process especially during the design phase, and then ultimately in the implementation phase. QoWS is first specified then published to be later on discovered by clients via the Web service interface description. QoWS is becoming a key differentiator in Web services competition as it allows the differentiation between providers of similar services. The provision of QoWS involves a number of QoWS management functions including QoWS specification, QoWS verification, QoWS negotiation and QoWS monitoring.

Nowadays, QoWS management for Web services is retaining considerable attention from Web services vendors, partners, and academia. Most research on QoS management has been performed in the context of delivering multimedia documents (e.g., video/audio streaming). QoWS management mechanisms were also applied to Web-based applications such as electronic commerce where users have access to online catalogues which may contain multimedia information. In the past recent years, research on Web services focused more on functional and interfacing issues, such as Simple Object Access Protocol (SOAP), Web Service Description Language (WSDL), and the Universal Description, Discovery, and Integration (UDDI). Most of today's Web services do not generally consider the level of QoWS they can deliver to their users. QoS support in Web services is still at the earlier stages of maturity as a research area where most of the efforts target the enumeration of QoWS requirements and mechanisms for QoWS management. Only recently, QoS issues began receiving more attention from the Web services community. QoWS is expected to become a value-added capability of emerging Web services as providers will be able to advertise in QoWS enabled registries to differentiate themselves from their competitors.

The need for QoS guarantee has been recognized as an important issue since the early stage of Web development. Web services add more challenges to the process of QoS guarantee since its context is dynamic and its environment is heterogeneous and continuously changing.

Currently, QoS for Web services is not managed in a well-structured manner and lacks management for important aspects such as QoWS certification, verification, negotiation, adaptation, composition, and renegotiation. The consideration of these key features for the success of any QoS management architecture raise many challenges as they are performed dynamically and may involve more than one participant.

The work presented in this thesis is concerned with Web services development (design methodology) and QoWS management for basic Web services together with composite Web services. A basic Web service is a Web service that provides alone a set of functionalities without relying on other Web services. A composite Web service is also known as the final Web service. The objective for such a Web service is to provide users with acceptable quality and cost-effective services. The definition of acceptable quality of service depends largely on the type of application and the user requirements in terms of Quality of Service.

The goal of this work is to develop a framework that provides a structured approach for Web service development which captures important characteristics of Web services regarding the QoWS management. The framework includes QoWS management operations for both service providers and consumers. Web services providers will be supported in the publication and verification of QoS rendered by their Web services while clients will be supported to express service specific requirements while selecting Web services. The quality of service management process within the framework is automatically conducted through a set of phases ranging from specification of QoWS parameters, selection of Web services driven QoWS, contract negotiation between providers and consumers, QoWS monitoring and guarantee, QoWS composition management.

1.3 Objectives

When this research was first started, the Web services paradigm was at its first stage of development and standardization where efforts were deployed particularly to define Web services concepts and enumerate their requirements. Service Oriented Architecture (SOA) was proposed to position the key players in this new paradigm. SOA defines the main operations executed within the components of this architecture. Technologies such as SOAP, WSDL, and UDDI were mainly designed to support these interactions. We believe that SOA and related technologies do not support a complete development process of Web services. It focuses more on defining the operations executed by each partner and the used protocols. In addition, these Web services technologies do not promise for Web services management and performance integration for Web services. Moreover, they do not support the QoWS composition management. We will study the possibility of developing a new framework that intends to capture all management operations stated previously. We look at the necessary extensions of SOA to support Web service management operations, QoWS management operations and QoWS composition management operations.

The aim of this thesis is to contribute toward the development of a generalized quality of Web service framework. To tackle this aim, an integrated Quality of Web Service Framework is designed to specify and implement QoWS management operations of basic and composite Web services.

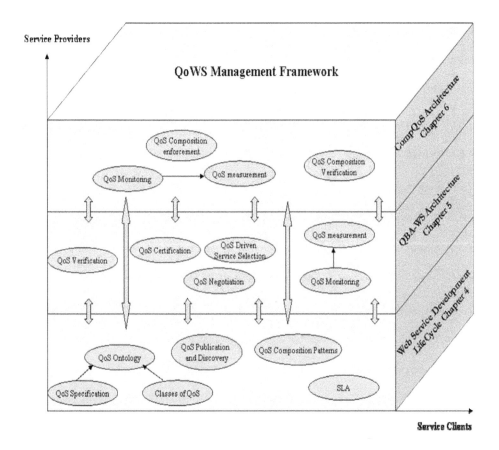

Figure 1 QoWS Management Framework

The framework presented in Figure 1 augments the SOA architecture to support QoWS

management and guarantee functions. These new operations will be offered to providers and

clients of Web services and are designed to fit into a highly dynamic and distributed

environment of Web services. Components of the framework are providing support for

verification, certification, selection, negotiation and monitoring of end-to-end QoWS for

basic and composite Web services.

In addition to the need for a richer Service Oriented Framework which allows the QoS

requirements of the new Web services to be fully specified, the Framework requires the

7

integration of a range of QoWS mechanisms in both providers' and clients' environments to meet end-to-end needs.

The proposed framework is divided into three layers:

- QoWS design methodology and patterns layer,

- QoWS management for basic Web service layer and

- QoWS management for composite Web service layer.

The first layer provides mechanisms that include design principals and methodology for QoWS specification, QoWS management, QoWS negotiation, and QoWS composition management. The second layer will offer operations of QoWS management for basic Web services mainly QoWS verification and certification, QoWS negotiation, and QoWS monitoring. The third layer will offer QoWS management operations for composite Web services essentially those related to verification and monitoring of QoWS composition.

The framework is developed using the bottom-up approach; therefore we start developing components of layer 1, then 2, and 3. Our first purpose was to define a new Web services development methodology that includes operations of Web services management, QoWS management, and QoWS composition management. Second, develop solutions for QoS management for basic Web services (Layer 2). Then, to develop solution for QoWS management of composite Web services (Layer 3). Management of composite Web services is more complex than the management of basic Web services. This complexity is implied by the fact that a composite Web service aggregates a set of basic Web services to provide a different, more complex service. In fact, in addition to the management of the composite Web service in its own, management of basic Web services must be performed accordingly and all management entities should share management information. Along with the development of the framework we identify challenges of QoWS management development operations, we propose solutions to these problems at both the conceptual and the implementation level, and we evaluate the applicability of these solutions on real Web services environment. The objectives of our research follow the three main dimensions (layers) which can be summarized in the following sub sections:

1.3.1 Web Services Development Lifecycle (methodology)

Our contributions to the development of a new Web services lifecycle are motivated from the point that the existing models do not fully capture all Web services activities. These activities concern QoWS management and QoWS composition management. Our approach was to investigate possibilities to augment the development process of Web services with the above important features.

The ultimate development methodology to design, implement, deploy, test, publish, discover, manage and compose Web services should give a great importance to the QoWS perception of the provider and the requester. The QoWS features are rather to be described in earlier phases through Web services development process especially during the design phase. These features concern QoWS specification, publication and discovery, and also composition and management design principals. The addressed design issues will help in future composition and management of Web services.

Existing Web services development models have the following limitation:

1. do not provide a detailed description of the design phase using, for example, existing modeling techniques as they are implementation or platform dependent;

2. they do not provide mechanisms to carry out important Web services features, such as QoWS management; and

3. they do not consider the maintenance of Web services throughout their life cycle.

Consequently, a new lifecycle will be proposed to outcome the above limitations. Supporting QoS in the description, publication, and discovery of Web services is needed for the success of any development lifecycle. These features will play a key role for distinguishing Web services and their providers. Web services design will be conducted following a precise modeling methodology. Design phase will support, in addition to the functional properties of Web services, the QoWS description and the specification of differentiated classes of QoWS. A QoWS class defines a set of quality parameters the Web service is able to support.

1.3.2 QoWS Management of Basic Web Services

Our contributions of this work according to the QoWS management are achieved through the development of QoWS *Broker* based architecture for management of QoWS. The architecture extends the SOA by introducing a new partner (mediator) who will be responsible for management and enforcement of QoWS. The requirements of this work regarding the QoWS management of basic Web service are summarized as follow:

1. Allow the definition of classes of QoWS to support increasing number of clients with different QoWS requirements. Well defined QoWS properties of Web services shall be made available and understandable to clients. The QoWS model shall provide an integrated view for both service providers and requestors, though they do not have the same view. The QoWS attributes are classified according to QoWS user requirements (different requirements for different users). Each class of service is described by the set of QoWS attributes each Web service can offer. Example of

QoWS attributes for Web services are: response time, availability, throughput, reputation, processing time, and cost.

2. Support QoWS description, QoWS publication and QoWS discovery. These processes require an extension of existing protocols and languages.

3. Provide support for QoWS management operations such as QoS-driven Web services selection, QoWS negotiation, QoWS verification and certification, and QoWS monitoring.

4. Achieve efficient selection and execution of Web services based on client requirements and QoWS verification and certification mechanisms.

5. Build a QoWS negotiation strategy that is supported through a negotiation protocol. The negotiation procedures allow both client and provider to reach an agreement on the level of QoWS supported by Web services. The negotiation is driven by an algorithm that is rule based and is executed by providers and/or clients.

6. Enable online monitoring of QoWS provision to assure compliance with published or negotiated QoWS requirements and provide immediate QoWS user feedback. The monitoring techniques consider mechanism for observing QoWS provision at runtime. These mechanisms start with gathering valuable information from the user and the provider of Web services for monitoring purposes. The QoWS monitoring technique use measurement based method to observe continuously the QoWS provided to the clients. Measurement consists of computing QoWS metrics in dynamic way and keep tracks on updated information about measurement.

7. Implement a prototype for each function performed within the architecture as proof of concept. This will assess and quantify the benefits and limitations of using QoWS

management architecture versus conducting QoWS management in a manual and ad-hoc manner.

Our research is an incremental research method in the sense that for each QoWS management operation, we study its feasibility, subsequently implement it, and then validate it. Validation is performed on real Web services environments and with close collaboration with other colleagues from other research groups.

1.3.3 QoWS Management for Composite Web Services

It is relatively easy to glue Web services together to provide the desired Web services functionalities, but it is difficult to guarantee the global QoWS provided by Web services made up of various Web services. Hence, it is critical to determine the distribution of a service property into its composed Web services and explain the global QoWS property from their individual Web services QoWS proprieties. Therefore, our primary goal was to develop a model that will guarantee the QoWS composition, its verification, and its monitoring. Verification and monitoring of QoWS composition will be very useful for both clients and providers. Clients will ensure that the composed Web service meets their QoWS requirements. On the other hand, the providers of composed Web services will be able to test and verify their QoWS composition before they publish it to clients.

The objectives of this work regarding the QoWS composition and monitoring of Web services are summarized as follow:

1. Define and apply a set of patterns for composing QoWS parameters of composed Web services.

2. Specify the set of QoWS composition patterns using an ontology that includes a categorization of the various patterns that may apply to a given QoWS composition.

3. Verify if the composed QoWS meets the overall QoWS composition requirements, with the fulfillment of QoWS composition patterns.

4. Use the verification of QoWS composition together with the client's requirements in selecting Web services to participate in composing a new Web service.

5. Define and formulate an ontology for classes of QoWS to facilitate the representation of QoS knowledge in the services interfaces of services partners.

6. Extend the interface description of a composed Web service with QoS composition information.

7. Support classes of QoWS composition of composite Web services: most of the solutions are restricting the QoWS composition to one type of QoWS for one category of clients. However, clients may have different and continuously changing QoWS requirements. The composition of QoWS classes wasn't considered before.

8. Maintain and update the composed QoWS values if the QoWS of one or more Web service partner changes (replacement, modification, or addition).

9. Support runtime monitoring of composite QoWS. Most of the existing solutions monitor the QoWS composition of the composite Web service without taking into consideration the monitoring of basic Web services. However, the violated QoWS may originate from the basic Web services and therefore, it will be more pertinent if the monitoring is carried out at different network locations, and monitoring information is gathered from different sources.

10. Evaluate the overhead induced by the QoS composition management in our solution. This aspect is often not studied. Some solutions can be very costly in terms of load generated due to the execution of each operation.

11. Monitor the behavior of all Web services partners (both composed and basic web services) to identify where the originated QoS violations occurred, and identify the Web services responsible for this violation.

Our solution to the above issues is developed within a support architecture, where a third party component will support QoWS management operations for composite Web services. For each QoWS operation, we study its feasibility, subsequently implement it, and then validate it. Validation is performed on real Web services environments.

1.4 Organization of the Thesis

The remainder of this thesis is organized as follows: Chapter 2 presents an overview of Web services and their related technologies. Then, it introduces the main definitions and concepts related to QoS in Web services. Moreover, it describes the most important QoWS management operations achieved within most of QoWS management architectures.

Chapter 3 presents a survey of the state of art on Web services lifecycles. Then, it reviews the background of QoS in the context of software, network, and distributed applications. Afterwards, it overviews related work on the QoWS management. It includes the description of most existing approaches and languages to specification of QoWS, and also an investigation of approaches to management of QoWS. Finally, a state of art on QoWS composition is presented and a summary of past results and remaining open issues are also presented.

In Chapter 4, we developed Web services lifecycles for better management of QoWS: one lifecycle for basic Web services and the other for composite Web services. These two different lifecycles aim to capture activities such as publication, discovery, management, performance, integration, and composition of QoWS. Prior to that and at the beginning of this chapter we describe existing initiatives for Web services development lifecycles, and we identify their limitations.

In Chapter 5, a broker-based architecture for QoWS management of basic Web services is described and the design of QoWS broker components is detailed. Afterward, a description of all QoWS management operations provided by the broker is presented, for instance QoWS verification, certification, negotiation, admission control, and monitoring operation. For, each QoWS operation the model used to conduct it is detailed and the algorithms that are executed within these models are also detailed and explained.

Chapter 6 addresses the challenges of QoWS management of composite Web service. It first, presents requirements of managing QoWS of composite Web services, and then it proposes and describes an ontology for classes of QoWS specification in the service interface description. Afterwards, a QoWS composition patterns are formalized and represented using XML. CompQoS architecture is proposed to manage the QoWS of composite Web services. Finally, a mobile driven mobile agent is used to monitor the QoWS of composite Web services.

Chapter 7 summarizes and presents the implementation conducted in this thesis. It first, describes the experimental prototype that we developed for the broker architecture proposed in this thesis. Then, it introduces prototype developed for the CompQoS architecture presented in chapter 6. The implementation includes the development of entities of these architectures and a complete validation of operations undertaken within the proposed architectures. A series of experimentation were conducted to evaluate the performance of Web services selection based on the QoWS and the client requirements. We also conducted a set of scenarios to validate and certify QoWS.

Chapter 8 concludes the thesis, highlight our contributions and potential future research directions.

Chapter 2

Web Services, QoWS: Terminology, Principles and Technologies

This chapter gives an overview of Web services and their related technologies. Then, it highlights the importance of SOA architecture and the benefits it provides over existing distributed system. Subsequently, it presents some limitations of the SOA-related standards and the issues they have to address in their future versions. Afterwards, the chapter summarizes terminology, principles, and concepts used in later discussions of QoWS. A specification of QoWS is described according to the points of view of providers and clients. Some related QoWS definitions are provided. Finally, descriptions of QoWS management operations in SOA are presented and a detailed description of each QoS management operation and an overview of how it is usually achieved are provided.

2.1 Introduction

There is an old debate on the meaning of the word "Quality". There is no general agreement on the definition of quality of service. The confusion behind the definition of this word is explained by the multitudes of existing definitions coming from different disciplines and domains. The evaluation of the quality of Web services is recognized as a multidimensional approach that is highly affected by many factors. These factors include the nature of the evaluated Web service, the evaluation environment and their attributes, and the perception of the involved actors (consumer, provider) toward the quality of Web service.

Next section will describe the SOA and the mainly technologies and protocols related to Web services.

2.2 Web Services and their Related Technologies Overview

2.2.1 Web Service Definition

A Service is the fact of serving or performing duties to clients. From another context, a service represents a set of functionalities that has an interface and can be called from programs or services. A service can also be located using service registry, to which services are registered. A service can be either an application service or a system service. An application service represents a user or a business activity (e.g. bill payment) and a system service represents infrastructure functionality (e.g. communication platform services). Large diversity of service technologies was developed to deal with interoperability for the purpose of efficient application integration, and the creation of uniform representation of applications within heterogeneous distributed systems COM [1], CORBA [2], EJB [3], RMI [4], and JINI [5]. Recently, a new variety of services has been developed: *Web Service*. Its goal is to deliver functionalities over the Internet.

Web services are an emerging technology that has attracted a lot of attention over the last few years. They are more and more used as a new paradigm for rendering services artifacts by handling queries issued over the Internet. Web services are interoperable across platforms and neutral to languages, which makes them appropriate for access from heterogeneous environments. With increasing acceptance among software vendors and rising adoption in the marketplace, Web services are becoming the basis for many Web-based applications. The objective is to reduce the complexity and expense of traditional business-to-business (B2B) connectivity. Web services technologies are based on open standards recommended by the World Wide Web Consortium (W3C). The standards enjoy unprecedented industry support from major IT suppliers such as IBM, Microsoft, and Sun Microsystems together with the foremost CORBA vendors, such as BEA, Borland and IONA Technologies.

Web services can be accessed using different protocols, different component models, running on different operating systems. Web services usually use Hypertext Transfer Protocol (HTTP) as a fundamental communication protocol which carries exchanged messages between clients and services. Web services use eXtensible Markup Language (XML) based messaging as a fundamental means of data communication. They also use new emerging standards for publication, discovery, and description.

Before Web services and these standards (i.e., SOAP, WSDL, and UDDI) came to the scene, connecting applications over a network was not an easy task. This is due to the fact that each application needs to have enough knowledge regarding the platform on which the other applications are running. This knowledge includes hardware, operating system, language, as well as the transport protocol to convey data between applications. Now, and by using Web services paradigm a common interface description, communication method, and message transport allow businesses to achieve the benefits of connecting over the Internet.

Many definitions of Web Services have been introduced in the literature. Some of them are incomplete and others are more detailed, more expressive and clearly explain the main properties of Web services. A more formal definition of a Web service may be borrowed from IBM's in [6].

"Web services are a new breed of Web application. They are self-contained, self-describing, modular applications that can be published, located, and invoked across the Web. Web services perform functions, which can be anything from simple requests to complicated business processes. Once a Web service is deployed, other applications (and other Web services) can discover and invoke the deployed service."

2.2.2 Web Services Architecture

The SOA defines a new component architectural concept that defines the use of Web services to satisfy software user's requirements. In a SOA environment, nodes on a network make resources available to other partners in the network as independent Web services that are accessible in a standardized way.

As depicted in Figure 2, the SOA is based on three operations and three roles communicating using a set of technologies. The three roles are the service provider, the service requester, and the service registry. The objects involved in the interactions between these roles are the Web service, and the service description. The operations performed by the actors on these objects are: publish, find, and bind.

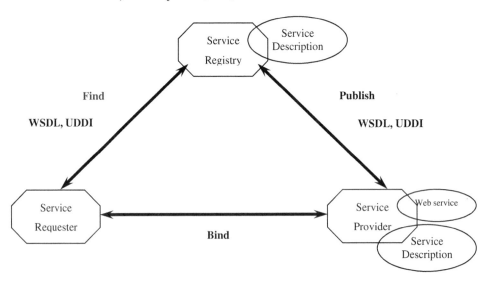

Figure 2 SOA Model

A service provider creates a Web service and its service description, using a standard called the Web Services Description Language (WSDL), and then publishes (Publish operation) this description in a service registry based on a standard called the Universal Description,

Discovery, and Integration (UDDI) specification. The service registry is a server that acts as a repository, or "yellow pages".

Once a Web service is published, a service requester may find the Web service by querying the UDDI interface (Find operation). The UDDI registry provides the service requester with a WSDL service description that holds the URL (uniform resource locator) pointing to the service itself. The service requester may then use this information to directly bind to the service (Bind operation).

SOA architecture stands on a family of protocols to describe, deliver, and interact with services. Next section will present these protocols that are recognized as Web services programming stack.

2.2.3 Web Services Programming Stack

The Web services protocol stack is a collection of standardized protocols and application programming interfaces (APIs) that are used to define, locate, implement, and make Web services interact with each other. The Web service protocol stack is mainly composite of four layers (you have also 3 towers):

1. Service Transport: This layer is responsible for transporting messages between network applications. It can be based on a HTTP, SMTP, FTP, as well as the more recent Blocks Extensible Exchange Protocol (BEEP) [7]. Other network protocols, such as the Internet Inter-ORB** Protocol (IIOP) [8] or the IBM MQSeries [9], can also be used.

2. XML Messaging: This layer is responsible for encoding messages in a common XML format so that messages can be understood at each end of the network connection. Actually, this area includes protocols such as XML-RPC [10], and SOAP [11]. All these protocols facilitate publish, find, and bind operations described previously.

3. Service Description. This layer is used for describing the public interface of a Web service. WSDL is typically used for this purpose. WSDL is often used in combination with SOAP and XML-Schema to provide Web services over the internet. A client, before connecting to a Web service, can parse the WSDL to find out what functions are published. Any user-defined data types used within the interfaces are embedded in the WSDL file in the form of XML-Schema. The client can then use SOAP to invoke one of the functions listed in the WSDL document.

4. Service Discovery: It centralizes services into a common registry such that Web services' providers can publish their description, and makes it easy to discover what services are available on the network. Nowadays, the UDDI protocol is normally used for Web services publication and discovery.

Web service protocol stack also includes a whole range of recently set up protocols (Figure 3): Web Services Flow Language (WSFL) [12], SOAP Security Extension: Digital Signature (SOAP-DSIG) [13], and Boniness Process Execution Language for Web Services BPEL4WS [14].

In order to meet the rigorous demands and requirements of today's e-business applications, an enterprise Web services infrastructure must be provided. This infrastructure should include, in addition to the above areas, security, management, and quality-of-service management. These infrastructure components, represented on the right side of Figure 3, have to be addressed at each layer of the stack. As the Web services paradigm is increasingly adopted throughout the industry, these issues are already undergoing standardization [15], [16]).

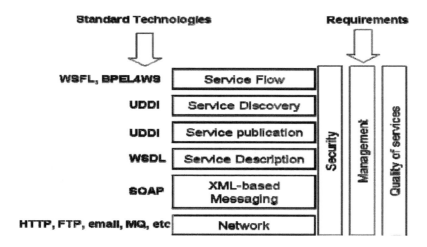

Figure 3 Web Services programming stack

In the following sub sections, a detailed description of most of the above protocols and languages mainly: SOAP, WSDL, UDDI, WSFL, and BPEL4WS is presented.

2.2.3.1 Simple Object Access Protocol (SOAP)

SOAP is an extensible, text-based framework for exchanging structured and typed information between peers, without prior knowledge of each other or of each other's platforms, in a decentralized, distributed environment using XML [11]. SOAP does not define any application semantics such as a programming model or implementation specific semantics, i.e., distributed garbage collection. It rather defines a simple mechanism for expressing application semantics by providing a modular packaging model and mechanisms for encoding data within modules [11]. This allows SOAP to be used in large variety of systems and software application environments. SOAP consists of three parts:

- A mandatory extensible envelope expressing what features and services are represented in a message; who should deal with them, and whether they are optional or mandatory. The envelope contains two elements: an optional header and a body.

23

- A set of optional encoding rules, which define a serialization mechanism that can be used to exchange instances of user-defined data types.

- An optional RPC representation, which defines a convention that can be used to represent the remote procedure calls and responses.

The following is a sample of a SOAP message based on HTTP as a network protocol.

```
POST /Accounts/xxxxx HTTP/1.1
Host: www.Webservicebank.com
Content-Length: nnnn
Content-Type: text/xml; charset="utf-8"
SOAPAction: "Some-URI"
<SOAP:Envelope xmlns:SOAP="http://schemas.xmlsoap.org/soap/envelope/"
  SOAP:encodingStyle="http://schemas.xmlsoap.org/soap/encoding/">
  <SOAP:Header>
    <t:Transaction xmlns:t="some-URI" SOAP:mustUnderstand="1">
        5
    </t:Transaction>
  </SOAP:Header>
  <SOAP:Body>
    <m:Deposit xmlns:m="Some-URI">
      <m:amount>200</m:amount>
    </m:Deposit>
  </SOAP:Body>
</SOAP:Envelope>
```

Figure 4 Sample of SOAP message

2.2.3.2 Web Services Description Language (WSDL)

The WSDL document describes where the Web service is located, what it can do, and how it can be invoked. The operations and messages are described abstractly, and then bound to a concrete network protocol and message format to define a network endpoint. Related concrete endpoints are combined into abstract endpoints. WSDL defines Web service as a collection of network endpoints (ports) [17]. The abstract definition of the endpoints and messages enables reuse of these definitions. A WSDL document uses the following elements when defining a Web service:

- Types – a container for data type definitions using some type system.

- Message – an abstract typed definition of the data being communicated.

- Operation – an abstract description of an action supported by the service.

- Port Type – an abstract set of operations supported by one or more endpoints.

- Bindings – a concrete protocol and data format specification for a particular port type.

- Port – a single endpoint defined as a combination of binding and a network address.

- Service – a collection of related endpoints.

While theoretically independent from SOAP and HTTP, WSDL is generally used with SOAP/HTTP as a remote invocation mechanism. Figure 5 presents an overview of WSDL document of a "WeatherSummary" Web Service published in [18].

```xml
<?xml version="1.0" encoding="UTF-8"?>
<definitions  name = "WeatherSummary"
     targetNamespace =  http://www.roguewave.com/soapworx/examples/WeatherSummary.wsdl >
  ......
  <types>
    <xsd:schema
      <xsd:element maxOccurs="1" minOccurs="1" name="sky"nillable="true" type="xsd:string"/>
      <xsd:element maxOccurs="1" minOccurs="1" name="temp" nillable="true" type="xsd:int"/>
    ......
    </xsd:schema>
  </types>
  <message name="getSummary">
    <part name="zipcode" type="xsd:string"/>
  </message>

  <message name="updateWeather">
    <part name="weatherData" type="wsx:WeatherSummary"/>
    <part name="port" type="xsd:string"/>
    <part name="transportName" type="xsd:string"/>
    <part name="weatherData" type="wsx:WeatherSummary"/>
  </message>
.....
  <portType name="WeatherSummary">
    <operation name="getSummary">
       <input message="tns:getSummary"/>
       <output message="tns:getSummaryResponse"/>
    </operation>
       .....
  </portType>
  <binding name="WeatherSummary" type="tns:WeatherSummary">
    <soap:binding style="rpc" transport="http://schemas.xmlsoap.org/soap/http"/>
      <operation name="getSummary">
        <soap:operation soapAction="getSummary"/>
        <input>
          <soap:body se="encoded"encodingStyle="http://schemas.xmlsoap.org/soap/encoding/"
                      namespace="http://www.roguewave.com/soapworx/examples"/>
          <soap:header message="tns:getSummary" part="header" use="literal"/>
        </input>
        <output>
          <soap:body se="encoded"encodingStyle="http://schemas.xmlsoap.org/soap/encoding/"
                    namespace="http://www.roguewave.com/soapworx/examples"/>
        </output>
      </operation>
      <operation name="updateWeather">  .....   </operation>
  </binding>
  <service name="WeatherSummary">
       <port name="WeatherSummary" binding="tns:WeatherSummary">
            <soap:address location="http://localhost:8090/weather/WeatherSummary"/>
       </port>
  </service>
</definitions>
```

Figure 5 Elements of WSDL description of WeatherSummary Web service

2.2.3.3 Universal Description, Discovery, and Integration (UDDI)

UDDI provides a mechanism for providers to publish Web services and for clients to dynamically find previously Web services [19]. The UDDI registry is similar to the CORBA trader service [20]. Clients of the UDDI registry can publish Web services, or search for Web services and bind programmatically to them. The UDDI registry consists of three sections (parts):

- the white pages that contain data on a business including address, contact, and known identifiers,
- the yellow pages that describe groups of related Web services; and
- the green pages that provide technical data about a given Web service, mainly to deal with how to connect to a Web service once it is found. The green pages hold references to specifications for Web services, as well as support for pointers to various file and URL based discovery mechanisms if required.

UDDI is layered on top of SOAP and assumes that requests/responses from/to UDDI objects are sent as SOAP messages.

2.2.3.4 Web Services Flow Language (WSFL)

Web Service Flow Language (WSFL) is an XML-based language for the description of Web Services Composition. Web services may be produced by composing existing Web services. Intra-enterprise Web services might collaborate to present a single Web service interface to the public, whereas Web services from different enterprises might collaborate to perform business to business transactions. A Web service flow describes how service-to-service communications, collaborations and flows are performed [12].

2.2.3.5 Business Process Execution Language for Web Services (BPEL4WS)

The Business Process Execution Language for Web services (BPEL4WS) represents the merging of IBM's WSFL and Microsoft's XLANG [21]. It is gaining a lot of interest and is positioned to become the primer standard for Web service composition. The BPEL4WS is used to specify business processes and business interaction protocols. It is an XML-based syntax which defines the interactions between a BPEL process and its partners via Web services interfaces. It also defines the state and the logic of coordination between these interactions as well as provides a way of handling exceptions [14]. This language makes the Web services composition process easier by providing concepts to represent partners and orchestrate their interactions.

In addition to BPEL4WS, WSFL, and XLANG, there are few standards that have been proposed in recent years. Sun, BEA, SAP, and Intalio have introduced another standard of Web services composition known as Web Service Choreography Interface (WSCI) [22].

2.2.4 The Importance of Web Services and their Technologies

Unlike traditional point-to-point architectures, SOA comprises loosely coupled, highly interoperable entities. The SOA architecture enhances the interoperability of distributed systems through the integration of independent languages and protocols that ease the publication, the discovery, and the binding of Web services. These Web services interoperate based on a formal definition independent from the underlying platform and programming language (e.g., WSDL). The interface definition hides the vendor and language-specific implementation and makes Web services very reusable since it is defined in a standards-compliant manner.

The rationale behind the success of SOA is the large support it got from all major IT vendors (IBM, HP, Oracle, Sun, etc.). Web services technology allows faster development, deployment, integration, and maintenance of business applications. Web services benefit from the adoption of widely known and used standards such as HTTP, XML along with other new XML-based standards(e.g. WSDL, and SOAP) to be easily accepted and adopted by companies. Web services technologies benefit from the experiences of previous distributed technologies such as CORBA distributed object, DCOM, EJB, RMI, JINI, etc.

High-level languages, such as BPEL or WS-Coordination [23], extend the Web service concept by providing a method for defining and supporting composition of Web services to create large scale Web services. These languages use the concept of workflow and provide features to represent partners and orchestrate their interactions. Proof

For all of the above motivations and others, the Web services concepts and technologies became one of the most important existing distributed computing standards and their adoption is expected to rise in the near future.

2.2.5 Some Limitations of Web Services Programming Languages and Protocols

Standard Web services protocols such as WSDL and UDDI were designed mainly for their functional features with only minor consideration for QoWS management, and QoWS composition management. Recently, considerable efforts have been conducted to tackle these issues. The trend in Web services management is to integrate QoWS support and management within the SOA. However, QoWS in SOA is highly linked to the QoWS of the application server on which the web services are deployed, the transport protocols (SOAP), the registry in which Web services are published and from which they are discovered, and the description language used to define the service interface (WSDL).

Little has been done for the QoWS in SOA architecture, until now most of the work is still under definition of requirements. Introducing QoWS in SOA can be done by either (1) extending the programming language and protocols stack part of SOA to support QoWS management and assurance for increasing numbers of clients with different requirements and/or (2) by developing new approaches and mechanisms to tackle the QoWS management by introducing a third party component that will be in charge of managing QoWS.

In addition to the above limitations regarding SOA architecture and their related technologies, a complete and structured way of developing Web services is needed. This ought to follow a sequence of phases which describes the process of developing Web services from the requirement definition to the maintenance of Web services.

2.3 Quality of Services Definition

Quality was early recognized in industry and academia, and then many definitions were proposed in the literature. A commonly used definition comes from the international quality standard ISO 8402 [24]: "*The totality of features and characteristics of a product or service that bear on its ability to satisfy stated or implied needs*". Quality of service as a related quality concern is defined in [25] as "*The collective effect of service performances which determine the degree of satisfaction of a user of the service*". QoS comprises a number of factors or attributes, which are enumerated and defined in the E.800 recommendation [25]. QoS of Web services concerns the non-functional aspects of the published Web service. This includes performance, reliability, availability, accessibility, etc. In SOA, both service providers and service users should be able to define and/or understand QoWS description to enable publication, discovery, and usage of QoWS attributes.

2.4 Quality of Web Services Terminology

In the list of QoWS related definitions presented bellow, some of them are referenced, others are not. Those that are not referenced were defined based on a deep analysis and discussion among our group and with other people from the field.

Quality: ISO 9000 defines quality as "degree to which a set of inherent characteristic fulfils requirements" [26].

Quality of Service (QoS): as defined is section 2.3 quality of service is the collective effect of service performances which determine the degree of satisfaction of a user of the service.

Quality of Web Services (QoWS): as defined is section 2.3 quality of Web service is the non-functional aspects of the published Web service.

Quality attributes: any feature or property of a software product, process, or resource that bears on its ability to satisfy stated and implied needs.

Quality View (Dimension): is the perception awarded to quality expression from different partners (e.g. consumer, provider, third party, etc.)

Quality Contract: describes the quality requirements of a client approved with the provider as formal agreement between both parties.

Class of QoWS: is a separate differentiation of the complete QoWS provided by one Web service.

Basic Web Service: a basic Web service is also known as a single Web service which provides alone a set of functionalities via a published interface description.

Composite Web Service: a composite Web service is also known as a final Web service and is an aggregation of more than one basic Web services to create more complex Web service with wide range of functionalities

Web Service Management: the management of a particular Web service or a group of Web services within the same application domain [27].

QoWS Management: is the set of operations that aim managing the QoWS between two or more parties, it includes QoWS agreement, QoWS monitoring, QoWS composition, QoWS negotiation, etc.

QoWS Composition: QoWS composition is to leverage, aggregate and bundle the individual Web services component's QoWS properties to derive the QoWS of the composite service component [28].

Web Services Client: is the entity that consumes the Web service, it is also known as the service requester, service user, service customer, and the service consumer.

2.5 QoWS Management Operations

Most work on QoWS management has been done in the context of multimedia distributed systems (e.g., delivery of video streams). QoWS issues were also considered in Web-based applications, such as electronic commerce, where users access online catalogues, which may contain multimedia information. Traditionally, QoWS provisioning is achieved through a number of phases that includes: QoWS specification, publication, discovery, negotiation, monitoring, mapping, degradation, admission control and resources reservation, adaptation, and termination. Following sub sections provide detailed insights of these phases.

2.5.1 QoWS Specification

QoWS specification is the first step in a sequence of required steps in QoWS management. QoWS description holds the specification of non-functional properties of Web services. This information can be specified in the Web service description interface. To commonly use the

QoWS specification by all Web services involved partners, it has to be supported by Web services architecture participants and their related technologies (e.g. SOAP, WSDL, and UDDI). To meet different clients' requirements, a classification of QoWS per categories or classes is considered; each class will describe different QoWS attributes and their related values.

2.5.2 QoWS Publication

As defined above, QoWS publication is the process that allows Web services providers to make publicly the Web services description available to the consumers. The Web service interface description holds, in addition to functional operations, the information about the non-functional aspects of the Web service. Therefore, the QoWS is described in the WSDL document and published through the UDDI registry. Web services technologies mainly WSDL, SOAP, and UDDI should support the QoWS description, transport, and publication.

2.5.3 QoWS Discovery

The QoWS discovery is the process that allows the consumers to search for Web services that meet their QoWS requirements. As defined in the publication process, the QoWS information extends the Web service interface. Hence, the service consumers specify their quality preferences while looking for Web services interfaces in the public registry. To support the QoWS while discovering Web services, standard Web services technologies (WSDL, SOAP, and UDDI) should handle the QoWS discovery.

2.5.4 QoWS Agreement (Negotiation)

The QoWS negotiation is the process of settling the level of QoWS the client is looking for, and the provider is able to deliver. This process can be conducted using a negotiation protocol and/or with the involvement of a third party negotiator. The negotiation is ended by an agreement or a disagreement on the QoWS that the Web services might support. If an agreement is reached, a QoWS contract is signed between concerned parties. The contract specifies generally what the provider should deliver, the guaranteed QoWS, and the cost.

2.5.5 QoWS Mapping

The QoWS can be presented differently from one level to another. For example, QoWS representation at the service level is different from the QoWS representation at the network level. The main objective of QoWS mapping is to provide an automatic and accurate translation of QoS properties between different levels. QoWS mapping between levels is a complex operation since the QoS parameters of a higher level is not often related to QoWS parameters of the lower level. However, the mapping procedures can not be considered as straightforward one-to-one QoWS attributes correspondence.

2.5.6 QoWS Measurement

Measurement is fundamental for dealing with quality. Indeed, quality should be computed prior to its evaluation and management. Measurement techniques could be applied to compute the QoWS metrics of a Web service either statically or at runtime. A metric defines a qualitative or quantitative property of the Web service that users want to evaluate. It is characterized by: Name, Data type, Type of element to be measured, and its computation logic. Examples of these metrics are response time, availability, reliability, reputation, and cost.

Quality metrics are useful in many aspects. A Web service can be selected based on the supported quality metrics: e.g. is it highly available, answers clients' requests in acceptable time, and has a good reputation. Furthermore, quality metrics will serve as the basis for adjusting the QoWS when it is violated. During process execution, the QoS needs to be monitored and checked against predefined and expected values. Whenever deviations are identified, dynamic adaptation mechanisms may be triggered.

2.5.7 QoWS Monitoring

QoWS monitoring of Web services is an important management activity which is required to support other management operations such as QoWS guarantee, QoWS adaptation, QoWS policing, and QoWS renegotiation. QoWS monitoring is the continuous, real time observation of the QoWS that is being provided. QoWS monitoring employs very often measurement techniques to compute dynamically the QoWS. The measured QoWS could be collected from different sources, including a third party monitor, user's feedbacks, and provider's notification. Once the measured value of a QoWS parameter does not meet the agreed one, violation is detected and announced, indicating the violation and if possible, the cause.

2.5.8 QoWS Admission Control and Resource Reservation

The admission control is the process of evaluating the resource required for the execution of requested QoWS and the available resources in the system, and then requests are admitted if resources are available. Once a request is allowed to use the services, resources could be reserved to meet the request requirements in terms of QoWS. This means that Web services access is denied to requests that cannot be completed within a certain desired level of

QoWS. Generally, admission control and resource reservation are performed based on the appliance of an admission control algorithm. The appliance of this algorithm decides whether the received requests are allowed to use a Web service.

2.5.9 QoWS Adaptation

The QoWS adaptation process is triggered once QoWS is violated (QoWS value goes below a threshold value). The role of QoWS adaptation is to maintain, as much as possible, the continuity of provisioning the Web service when the initially contracted QoWS is no longer supported. Adaptation procedures are various, and can affect one or more QoWS parameters. The adaptation process is initiated based on a set of detected violations by the monitoring procedures. The provider uses a multitude of techniques to adapt the violated QoWS to a level agreed or acceptable by the client. These techniques range from implementing server selection policies, dynamic server instantiation, to differentiated classes provision of Web services. In the first technique, policies are implemented at the server side to adapt the QoWS by delaying requests that have lowest priority and accepting those of highest priority. The second techniques allow the addition and removal of servers according to demand and that offer the support for load distribution. The third technique is based on differentiating between requests based on a specific classification and selecting Web servers according to this classification.

2.5.10 QoWS Termination and Billing

Once the Web service provision is terminated, the reserved resources are released and a bill is prepared for the client. Messages must be exchanged between the two intervening roles in QoS management (Web service provider and client) to terminate the QoS provision.

2.6 Summary

This chapter attempted to cover most of terminologies, features, and operations related to web services and QoWS. The QoWS vocabulary is very large, and was studied in many domains (e.g. networking, distributed systems, and Web applications). Thus, this chapter tried to give an overview of the most important features that is gaining high interest in our research on QoS for Web services. Additionally, it tried to cover the terminologies traditionally used in the context of QoWS specification and management that will be used all along this thesis. Moreover, it described the most important operations of QoWS management.

While this chapter introduces the main technologies and principals related to Web services and to the QoWS management; the next chapter will present the state of art of Web services development methodologies, QoWS management, and QoWS composition management.

Chapter 3
Related Work

In this chapter, we will survey the most relevant previous works on Web services development lifecycles and QoWS management for Web services. We will also compare and contrast to those closest to our work. This chapter will be organized as follows: we will first survey QoWS management in software, network, and in distributed environments. Afterwards, we will present and discuss the most relevant work on Web services development models, and QoWS management. These will include a review of some existing languages for QoWS specification, a discussion of the solutions for QoWS management from both academia and industry. Furthermore, we will go over (review) the most important work on QoWS composition management. Finally, we will summarize the context of previous work and identify the remaining open issues in QoWS management for Web services.

3.1 Introduction

The adoption of Web services by both industry and academic researchers leads to the proposition of solutions that progress along different dimensions. Academic research has been mostly concerned with expressiveness of Web services description, while industry has focused on Web services languages, protocols and architectures.

With the proliferation of Web services and their wide adoption as novel technology for business- to-business interactions on the Web, QoWS management has been generating a considerable interest in recent years.

3.2 Literature Review

In this section, we will survey the most important existing work, those that are closest to our work, especially those related to: Web services lifecycle, QoS management in distributed system and network, and QoWS management of basic and composite Web services.

3.2.1 Web Service Development Lifecycle

A Web Services Development Lifecycle (WSDLC) is the series of steps through which a Web service progresses from the early requirement definition phase until maintenance and retirement of a Web service.

Only few Web services research groups worked on WSDLC. IBM, HP and Sun Microsystems Web services working groups have defined proposals for Web services development models that guide developers in their development process.

IBM Web services working group has defined a high level description of a WSDLC. The proposed lifecycle aim's to facilitate, for developers, the adaptation of SOA to Web services development process. The proposed model identifies four common design and development scenarios [29]: Green field, bottom up, top down, and meet in the middle scenario. These scenarios describe, in a high level, the process of Web services development without being worried about description details of each phase. The main focus is how to build Web services, from scratch, from existing applications, or from combining both approaches. However, many fundamental features related to Web services design, composition, management, and maintenance is missing. Also, QoWS is not integrated in the description, the publication and discovery of Web services.

S. Williams and K. Brennan from HP working group defined a WSDLC as the developer's assistant to build Web services based solutions. This lifecycle is decomposed into nine primary steps or areas of concern that are followed in the specified order [30]:

- Define or obtain public business processes.

- Program public Web service interfaces.

- Construct business object and data.

- Build workflows.

- Map public interfaces.

- Package the services.

- Deploy the services.

- Advertise services.

- Monitor running Web services.

During every phase, description details are provided, and supporting tools and protocols are defined. Compared to IBM model, the HP model is described in more details. However, its main drawback relates to its high level of coupling to HP platform and tools. Moreover, it does not recognize the importance of design, composition, management, maintenance, and QoWS.

Sun Microsystems describes a model for Web services life cycle with a particular emphasis on management patterns of Web services [31]. The proposed model identifies the features and attributes of managing production-quality Web services based on the proposed lifecycle. This life cycle is divided into four phases, namely: design & build, test, deploy & execute, and manage. Sun WSDLC has the advantage of performing management all over the lifecycle phases. However, the model does not consider composition, QoWS, and maintenance of Web services.

The three WSDLCs described above are not yet validated. They are considered as a first initiative towards future adoption. In fact, the Web services development process involves more phases and management mechanisms due to the heterogeneous environment of Web services. These requirements concern data analysis, information structuring, Web services management, Web services composition, Web services versioning, reliable messaging, security, performance, and QoWS. Some of these characteristics are not considered in the design and the implementation of Web services when using existing WSDLCs. Furthermore; these WSDLCs are tied too closely to the architecture, development tools, programming language and the vendor support. They emphasize more on the implementation phase compared to the design phase.

The existing models do not provide a formal description of the design phase (a key phase in WSDLC) using, for example, existing modeling techniques. This is due to the fact that they are implementation/platform-dependent. They do not provide mechanisms to carry out important Web services quality characteristics, such as QoWS support. Furthermore, they do not consider the maintenance of Web services throughout their lifecycle.

Consequently, a new WSDLC should be developed to solve the above limitations and supporting description, publication, and discovery of QoWS. This is particularly needed for the success of any WSDLC. In fact, these features will play a key role for distinguishing Web services providers. Web services design should be conducted by a modeling methodology. Design phase should support in addition to Web services functions, the QoWS description, and the definition of differentiated classes of QoWS. A class of QoWS defines a set of quality parameters the Web service is able to support.

The implementation phase does not provide information for Web services clients about operations such as copying, moving, deleting, or upgrading Web services. These operations are supposed to be part of the implementation phase of Web services development. Furthermore, the maintenance of Web services is not explicitly considered in these models even though this phase is of critical importance given the high cost of maintaining Web services and software in general.

Management of Web services is a key concern in Web services lifecycle. In software lifecycle, management is limited in its scope due generally to the static nature of software and its closed environment. Web services management depends on many factors: time, open distributed environment, multiple protocols, and diverse clients' profiles. Management should be involved all over WSDLC, and ought to cover fault management, execution management, and composition management.

Web services composition is also an important issue that needs to be developed as an independent phase of Web services lifecycle. Web services have to be designed to participate in its management and in the way to compose another Web service. For this purpose, interfaces should be developed to help in management, and composition of Web services.

The maintenance of Web services is needed to correct and/or enhance Web services to support new functional/non-functional features.

3.2.2 Existing Research on QoS Management

Since QoS has been largely studied in the area of software engineering, network management, and distributed applications and systems, a considerable work has been developed. In the following sub section, we overview some of these works and we relate, and compare them to the QoS management in the context of Web services.

3.2.2.1 QoS Management in Software Component and Web Application

Many software products and Web sites quality models have been proposed and have different goals and approaches. They can be classified as: Mathematical based models or Artificial Intelligence-based models ([32], [33], [34]). In the context of Web services, considerable attention was brought to the QoS support. Therefore, a number of works were proposed to categorize, specify, measure, and evaluate QoS for Web services ([35], [36], [37], [38], [39]).

Modeling QoS for Web services is in general similar to modeling quality for software products. According to [40], there are two approaches to model product quality: fixed model and define-your-own model. The existing fixed model for software or component quality evaluation, such as approaches, referred in [41] provides a fixed set of quality characteristics. In the second approach, the model reflects the organization context and the QoS perceived by the quality model developers. The Quality view (goals, requirements) may differ from an organization to another and even among users in the same organization.

3.2.2.2 QoS Management in Network Infrastructure

QoS from networking point of view refers to the capability of a network to provide an acceptable service to selected network traffic over one or heterogeneous networks (e.g. IP-based, ATM, VoIP, etc.). Supporting end-to-end QoS through the network was widely covered in literature and industry. Hence, diverse solutions were developed to implement QoS support at the network infrastructure. Integrated Services (IntServ) [43], Differentiated

Services (DiffServ) [44], Multi Protocol Label Switching (MPLS) [45], and Bandwidth Broker for DiffServ Networks [46] are all technologies used to guarantee the QoS at the network layer.

Users use the Internet to invoke Web services. Currently, the Internet delivers all traffic equally as "Best Effort" and provides no support for QoS. Supporting QoS between Web services and their clients cannot be delivered while neglecting the QoS at the underlying network connecting both parties. QoS of Web services have to include network properties according to the public network (i.e. Internet). Specific QoS attributes for networks are bandwidth, delay, jitter, latency, and loss of characteristics.

3.2.2.3 QoS Management Architectures for Distributed Systems

QoS management in distributed systems was among the hot topics that have received great interest in the past few years. Many architectures have been proposed to manage the QoS for distributed applications ([47], [48], [49], [50]). The main objectives of these architectures are to define a set of configurable quality of service interfaces to formalize QoS in end-system and networks. These architectures provide and integrate QoS control and management mechanisms.

The majority of approaches for QoS management in distributed applications are presented in ([47], [48]) as follow:

- Extended Integrated Reference Model (XRM), which is being developed at Columbia University;

- Quality of Service Architecture (QoS-A), which is being developed at Lancaster University;

- OSI QoS Framework, which is being developed by the ISO SC21 QoS Working Group;

- Heidelberg QoS Model, which is being developed at IBM's European Networking Center;

- TINA QoS Framework, which is being developed by the TINA Consortium;

- IETF QoS Manager (QM), which is being developed by the IETF Integrated Services Working Group;

- Tenet Architecture, which is being developed at the University of California at Berkley;

- OMEGA Architecture, which is being developed at the University of Pennsylvania; and

- End System QoS Framework, which is being developed at Washington University.

These architectures and frameworks may be classified into two classes according to the scope of the components considered (network component, and end-system component). For example, the Tenet architecture [50] considers the QoS at the communication system level, while other architectures, like for instance the QOS-A architecture from Lancaster University [48], includes end-system components. A detailed survey of existing QoS architectures is given in [47].

There is still more work to be done in order to come up with comprehensive QoS architectures for distributed systems that will incorporate QoS interface, control, adaptation, and management across all architectural layers.

3.2.3 QoS Management of Basic Web Services

To evaluate quality of Web services, it is necessary to define quality attributes. These attributes are used as criteria to discriminate high quality Web service. Many quality attributes have been proposed in software engineering ([33], [34], [40], [41]) however, they are insufficient to cover all the important aspects of Web services. For example the dynamic nature of Web services and its business perspective involves new quality properties such as availability, thrust, and reputation. These properties are often not considered for software and component. Common quality attributes are efficiency, functionality, portability, reliability, usability, maintainability, expandability, interoperability, reusability, integrity, survivability, correctness, verifiability, flexibility, performance, dependability, security, and safety [42]. Few works on Web services QoS classification are presented in ([36], [38]). Their focus is on the classification of QoS supported attributes, but they do not define how these QoS will be supported at the Web service description, publication and discovery.

Other than, there has been a considerable amount of research work, approaches, architectures, and industrial tools for QoS management for Web services. Although, it is not possible to cover in detail all of this interesting work, we will highlight the most relevant of them; and the widely adopted approaches, those related to the topics discussed in this thesis. In sub sections, we will start first by presenting some approaches and languages for specification of QoS for Web services, since it is the first phase towards QoS management. Then, we will survey solutions from research and industry field proposed for management of QoS for Web services. Finally, we will present some industrial tools developed to support QoS management for Web services.

3.2.3.1 Approaches and Languages for Specification of QoWS

The process of QoWS management is conducted always through a set of phases. Specifying QoWS is the first phase in QoWS management. This phase is an inevitable required process prior to QoWS management. It consists of describing and defining QoWS information that will be used to constitute a formal agreement between both parties: clients of Web services and provider of Web services. QoWS description is captured to be used in other QoWS operations such as QoWS publication, discovery, and monitoring.

There is a considerable work from the software engineering area on the formal representation of various types of constraints in multimedia application such as the Hierarchical QoS Markup Language (HQML). As well, other languages are developed for Quality of Service Specification in distributed object systems for example: the QoS modeling language (QML), and the Quality Description Languages (QDL). These languages cannot be reused for the specification of QoWS due to the following factors: (1) Incompatibility with Web services standard (e.g. WSDL, SOAP, and UDDI). (2) Lack of interoperability of Web services implementations and interaction method used (asynchronous, RPC, etc.). (3) And the dynamic aspect of Web services selection and composition [51].

In the literature, considerable efforts have been conducted to specify QoWS. We will present hereafter only those that are standardized and widely used. DAML-S provides an upper ontology for semantic description of Web services, including specification of functionalities and QoWS constraints [52]. IBM proposes Web Service Level Agreements (WSLA), which is an XML specification of SLAs for Web Services, focusing on QoWS constraints [53]. Web Service Offerings Language (WSOL) has been developed for the formal specification of various constraints, management statements, and classes of services for Web Services [54].

47

Also, new specifications of Web Services (WS-* specifications) [55] are being proposed to incorporate transactions, reliable messaging, security, interoperability, quality of service, orchestration and choreography, some of them ([56], [57], [58], [59]) are already undergoing standardization.

3.2.3.2 Approaches for measurements and monitoring of QoWS

Monitoring the QoWS is an important activity required to support other QoWS management functions, such as QoWS adaptation and QoWS policing. It consists of observing the provision of QoWS between clients and their providers in order to detect any violations of the initially agreed QoWS. Several approaches have been investigated in the literature to deal with QoWS monitoring. Most of them have been applied to distributed multimedia applications, network services, and Web-based applications such as electronic commerce ([60], [61], [62], [63], [64], [65], [66]). The work presented in [67] provides and analyses the challenges and approaches used to provide support for QoWS monitoring in distributed and network environments.

Different techniques were used to monitor QoS in distributed applications and Web services. They range from measurement based approach[68] , framework-based Web service monitoring [69], and mobile agent-based observers for Web services monitoring [70].

Monitoring QoWS for Web services relies on an entity that gathers accurate measurements, models and analyses the data over certain periods of time or when specific events happen. Monitoring QoWS is highly affected by the Internet infrastructure as Web services are deployed and consumed via the Internet that is known as an unreliable network environment. These characteristics make QoWS monitoring of Web services difficult to automate and manage.

QoWS measurement is an important phase usually used as part of QoWS monitoring. It consists of defining a set of procedures for computing at runtime the QoWS attributes. Measuring QoWS attributes of Web services is not an easy task. The dynamic nature of the Internet and the autonomy of Web services make the measurement process awfully difficult. Restricting measurements of QoWS to the server site is not effective because of the unpredictable nature of the Internet. In the heterogeneous environment of Web services, it is more meaningful to perform measurements at different locations including the provider and the client sides. For example, evaluating QoWS parameters, such as response time, at the server side has little significance for the client because it excludes the round-trip propagation time of the request and its response. Another issue concerns monitoring QoWS of composite Web services, Web services that use other available Web services to answer the client's requests. In this case, monitoring composite Web services is more and more complex due to the involvement of multiple components from different locations. In next chapter, we discuss our solution to deal with this issue.

3.2.3.3 Approaches for Management of QoWS

As Web services approach is a recent paradigm, most of the work in the area focuses on the development and deployment of Web services. Management of Web services and in particular QoWS management is still not a mature area. Proposals are still emerging and architectures (approaches) for Web services and QoWS management are still under experimentation. Solutions for QoWS management of Web services can be divided into two categories. The first category has been emerged from research community and the second category presents solutions from industry.

3.2.3.4 Research Solutions Toward Management of QoWS

In the literature, the approaches that have been proposed to provide QoWS support and management for Web services can be classified into two categories: (1) approaches that enhance the existing Web service protocols such as UDDI, SOAP, and WSDL to support QoWS operations, and (2) approaches that use an independent brokerage Web service that will be in charge of supporting of all or some of the QoS operations.

Among work belonging to the first category, SOAP extension approach extends the SOAP header to include QoWS information [69]. WSDL extension approach augments the WSDL document with QoWS annotations. These annotations describe each QoWS parameter, its associated value, and its computation unit (e.g. millisecond, request/second). UDDI extension approach consists in extending the current UDDI data structure with QoWS information [71]. Extensions are relatively simple and QoWS publication and discovery will be achieved within the Web services publication and discovery. Some limitations of the above approaches can be: (1) the QoWS specification will be too tied to the Web services protocol and languages, (2) the extension mechanisms are not standardized, (3) Run-time update of QoWS information requires updates of the affected copy of WSDL files, which is not easy.

In the second category of work mentioned in the beginning of this section, numerous efforts have been made for managing QoWS. This work presents solutions for at least one of the following QoWS management operations: QoWS verification, QoWS discovery and selection, QoWS negotiation, QoWS monitoring, and QoWS control and adaptation.

Related approaches for QoWS-driven Web services discovery, selection, and verification are proposed initially by Shuping Ran in [38]. The author proposes a generic model for Web services discovery that includes the functional and non-functional requirements of Web services (i.e. QoWS). The model proposes certifying QoWS claims to the providers and verifies these QoWS claims for the clients. The introduced certifier is not well defined and not implemented; it does not describe the details of the certification process; furthermore, it neither verifies the WSDL content nor controls the delivery of the selected QoWS.

On the same direction, Sravanthi et al presented in [72] a broker-based architecture for verity and reputation in SLA-enabled Web services. The authors defined "verity" as the ability to maintain the lowest difference between the projected and achieved levels of service. Using their model, they argued that compliance and verity are the more intuitive indicators of the providers' trustworthiness. The main limitation of this work is the lack of verification and certification of Web services and their QoWS. The proposed verity and compliance metrics are computed at runtime when the Web service is invoked without any verification made in advance either on the Web service description or on its offered QoWS attributes.

Tsai et al. suggested in [73] test scripts specification techniques to perform testing within the UDDI server. Test scripts should be attached to each Web service to be used by both Web service providers and clients to test Web services before the publication or discovery process. Web services are accepted only if tests are successful. The verification tests are performed in UDDI registry that does not support QoS-aware Web services publication and discovery.

With main focus on addressing the issue of Web service selection, Maximilien et al. propose a framework and ontology for dynamic Web services selection in [74]. The framework incorporates service selection agents that use the QoWS ontology and an XML policy language that allows service consumers and providers to expose their quality preferences and advertisements. It lets providers, consumers, and agents to collaborate to determine each other's Web service quality and trustworthiness. In addition to the usage of software agent that helps in Web services selection, this approach contributes in implementing QoWS ontology. This ontology allows all participants of the framework to express and exchange, in common way, their quality constraints. Still this work has the limitation of trusting each other's quality information. A malfeasant agent may behave improperly and deliver wrong information to other partners. Also, the amount of information (messages) exchanged between involved parties may overwhelm them with extra load (data) and thus suffer a quality degradation.

Zhang et al. presented in [75] an approach that facilitates reliability testing of Web services. They tried to address the following questions: How to effectively and efficiently test remote Web services? How to test the reliability of remote Web Services? And how to test the interoperability of remote Web service in software based environment? To answer these questions, the proposed model uses a mobile agent which assists service requestors to select appropriate and reliable Web services. A prior remote testing is made using SOAP message through Web services interface. The approach applies fault injection and assertion to Web services components selection. The main advantage of using agents is to eliminate both network traffic and transport protection overhead. The presented model is generic and lacks technical details about the implementation and the complexity that may be generated. A validation of the model is its major limitation. Therefore, a real validation through an implementation and/or simulations is of high importance to evaluate the features of the proposed model.

There are also some research efforts that address the issue of testing and verifying Web services composition. Tsai et al. presented in [76] a Web services group testing to test composite Web services. The approach involves the collaboration and cooperation of all parties to perform testing. The voting procedures are done in real time at both unit and integration levels. Technical details about the implementation and its requirement are the main weaknesses of this work. Also, collaboration of all parties in testing composite Web service involves the issue of extra load generated from the exchanged information between them; this issue is not considered and evaluated by the proposed model.

Chen et al presented in [77] a description and an implementation of broker-based architecture for controlling QoS of Web services. The broker acts as an intermediary third party to make Web services selection and QoS negotiation on behalf of the client. Delegation of selection and negotiation to a third party raises trustworthiness issues mainly for clients. Moreover, performance of the broker is not discussed. However, performance of the broker is of critical importance to the success of any proposed broker-based architecture. If the user does not get a response to his/her request within an acceptable period of time, he/she will switch to another provider. Some similar broker-based architectures have been presented in [78] and [79]; they focus more on the QoS specification using XML schema, and dynamic QoS mapping between Web server and network performance.

In [80], the authors propose a model for dynamic Web services selection that is performed at both the client and the provider side. The service providers can request the services offered by other providers. The authors investigate three approaches for retrieving status information from service providers: an RPC-based approach, a mobile agent-based approach, and a circulating mobile agents approach. They validate these tree models using a quantitative analysis.

The drawback of most of the proposed models for Web services selection is that they consider an intelligent client, able to retrieve status information from service providers and rank them according to its constraints and QoS requirements.

In [81], the authors describe an agent-based approach for service selection in Web services. This approach borrows interesting elements from conventional approaches for selection, like collaborative filtering and reputation system. It is based on the collaboration among agents to evaluate service providers. Besides, agents autonomously decide on how much to weight each other's recommendations.

In summary, the solutions presented above for QoWS management present some substantial limitations. These limitations are related to one or more of the following issues:

- Most of the QoWS operations performed are often restricted to Web services selection operation based on QoWS. Even so, other management operations such as QoWS verification and certification, QoWS negotiation, QoWS monitoring, and QoWS adaptation are also needed.

- None of these solutions considers the performance of the entity responsible of managing QoWS (e.g. Broker). However, the performance of the broker can affect the whole architecture if it is not behaving as expected.

- The brokers that mediate between the client and the provider behave totally on behalf of clients in selecting Web services. As the consumer lacks the knowledge about the broker and provider of the Web service. The challenge arises the consumer may not be able to trust the service broker.

- Supporting classes of Web services is not considered in most of the proposed solutions. Most of solutions are restricting the provider in delivering services to one category of clients. However, clients may have different and continuously changing requirements.

- The monitoring operations proposed in the above solutions for QoWS management of Web services are often performed on one location and involve frequently one component. Therefore, it will be more interesting if the monitoring information is combined from different sources and performed at different locations.

- The cost evaluation of each solution for QoWS management of Web services is often not studied. For example, some solutions can be very costly in terms of load generated due to the execution of each management operation, and also in terms of software and/or hardware required resources for the deployment and the configuration of the adopted solution.

3.2.3.5 Industrial Solutions for Management of QoWS

Among work on QoS management for Web services, a considerable number of management tools have been developed to be integrated into Web services environments. For example, the HP Web services Management Engine (OpenView) [82] allows to perform management operations for Web services as well as the definition and the enforcement of Service Level Agreement (SLA). The Parasoft platform [83] offers a set of tools (SOAPTest, TEST, Webking) to support management during the Web services development process. The IBM

Tivoli management framework [84] includes a business systems manager component to carry out management operations.

These management frameworks differ in terms of the QoS parameters considered and in the way the management tasks are performed. Now, most of the management infrastructures for Web services are moving towards the integration of the QoS management within the service oriented architecture. An example of these infrastructures is the OASIS Web Services Distributed Management (WSDM) [85] and the WS-Management from Microsoft [86]. Some issues such as scalability, QoS guarantee, and high availability of Web services are still less considered in the above frameworks. These features will add value to the emerging architectures for QoS management in Web services.

3.2.4 QoS Management of Composite Web Services

Web services composition has generated a considerable interest in recent years ([87], [88], [89]). Most work focused mainly on the composition of Web services and their related issues. Also, standards and/or languages were proposed with the purpose of helping the composition of Web services. These include: WSFL [12], DAML-S [52], WCSL [90], BPEL4WS [13], and Web WSCI [22]. These languages facilitate the Web services composition process and make easier their interactions. Among these technologies, BPEL4WS, which represents the merging of IBM's WSFL and Microsoft's XLANG, is becoming a wide adopted standard for Web services composition. For this reason, BPEL is used in our work and then will be considered in the remaining chapters of this thesis.

Nowadays, research initiatives have been carried out to tackle the issue of management of QoWS composition of a composite Web service. Michael C. Jaeger et al. in [91] and [92] focus on defining and extending abstract composition patterns with consideration on Web services dependencies. Also, they propose to use the pattern-based aggregation in the monitoring process during run time. The proposed model is a generic model that requires technical details about the implementation and the complexity it generates. The model does not describe the monitoring process of a composite Web service or how monitoring of QoS is conducted. On the same direction, Cardoso et al. [93] proposed a mathematical model for QoS aggregation in workflow. The model applies a QoS computation algorithm that uses a set of reduction patterns to the workflow in order to obtain a valid and final workflow task. Zeng et al. in [94] proposed a QoS-based framework for selecting Web services partners while building composite Web services. The model evaluates the overall QoS of Web services using a local optimization approach and a global planning approach. These approaches are used for selecting Web services that will execute a specific task in the composition. Canfora et al. in [95] proposed an approach to trigger and perform composite service replanning during execution. Replanning is triggered as soon as it is possible to predict the actual Web service QoS, and detect if it will deviate from the initial estimate. Then, the part of the Web service flow that still has to be executed will be determined and replanned. The approach relies on a proxy-based architecture to easily permit the binding between abstract and concrete Web services, as well as to perform replanning.

Tao et al. in [96] proposed a broker-based framework to facilitate dynamic integration and adaptation of QoS-aware Web services with end-to-end QoS constraints. Their work focuses more on defining the Web services selection and composition model to compose and adjust the business process to meet users' requirements in terms of QoS. The paper focuses more on the composition by creating process execution plans and uses a selection algorithm to select the best path in a workflow for the business process request. An adaptation approach is executed to adapt the process execution by selecting backup path whenever a failure occurs. The work does not consider the validation, enforcement, and the monitoring of the QoS composition. However, QoS composition should be monitored at run-time to check whether individual QoS complies with the contract and the whole composite QoS is maintained.

Baresi et al. in [97] presented an approach for monitoring the execution of composite Web services. The BPEL process is annotated by the provider of composite Web service using assertions, but there is no prior validation of these annotations. The monitoring conducted aims to assess the correctness of Web services composition. It focuses only on the monitoring of functional contract, the timeout, and exception handling.

With reference to the above solutions for QoS composition management of composite Web services, there are still some important issues to be addressed. In fact, to enable a reliable and trustable QoS composition, we need a dynamic framework to verify and monitor the QoS composition. This framework should address and implement the following features:

- Support composition of classes of QoS in Web services: most of the above solutions are restricting the QoS composition to one type of QoS for one category of clients. However, clients may have different and continuously changing QoS requirements. None of the approaches consider the composition of classes of QoS.

- Validate the QoWS composition to both clients and providers before and after selecting a composite Web service.

- Ensure the continuous verification of QoS composition while maintaining the QoS requirements of clients.

- Use the verification of QoS composition together with the client's requirements in selecting Web services to participate in composing a Web service.

- Support runtime distributed monitoring of composite QoS and participating Web services. Most of the proposed solutions monitor the QoS composition at the final Web service. However, a violated QoS by the composite Web service may be caused by a basic Web service. Therefore, it will be more pertinent if the monitoring is performed at different locations, and information is collected from different sources.

- Verification of QoWS composition will be very useful for both clients and providers. Clients will ensure that the composite Web service meets their QoS requirements. On the other hand, the providers of composite Web services will test and verify their QoS composition before they publish it to clients.

- The monitoring of a final Web service and basic Web services will locate where the originated QoS violations occurred, and identifies the Web services responsible of this violation. Thus, the QoS of responsible Web services will be adapted, or they will be even replaced.

- The overhead of the management of QoS composition of Web services is often not studied, and by the way not estimated. For example, some solutions can be very costly in terms of generated load due to the execution of each operation.

3.3 Summary

This chapter tried to provide an overview of the most important work on Web services development methodologies and QoWS management. It first presented the existing initiatives of Web services lifecycles and reviewed some of their limitations. Then, it presented existing approaches for QoWS-aware Web service selection, QoWS based Web services publication and discovery, QoWS negotiation, QoWS monitoring, and QoWS composition of composite Web services. Also, the chapter enumerated limitations of existing approaches for QoWS management. Afterwards, it addresses the remaining QoWS management issues that still to be tackled in future solution for QoWS management.

The next chapter will present a Web services development lifecycles of basic and composite Web services that tackles the QoWS management issues addressed in this chapter, especially the QoWS management operations integration in Web services lifecycle, and the QoWS composition management.

Chapter 4
Toward a New Approach for Web Services Development
Lifecycle (Methodology)

In this chapter, we propose a new development lifecycle for Web services[1]. This WSDLC overcomes the limitations of previously presented approaches. It is a structured model that can be used as the basis for defining a systematic approach to the development of Web services.

The remainder of the chapter is organized as follows: we will first survey the features of software and component development lifecycle, and describe the common phases they undertake. Then, we discuss the existing WSDLC limitations based on the description of these lifecycles stated in chapter 3. Afterwards, we describe our proposed approach for WSDLC of basic Web services showing all details of its phases. We then, demonstrate that a composite Web service needs a separate lifecycle. Therefore, we propose a lifecycle for composite Web services and we describe each of their phases. Finally, we summarize the chapter and we point to remaining future work.

The implemented features of the lifecycles proposed in this chapter are evaluated in chapter 5, 6, and 7. A prototype of a video Web service is implemented using the model presented in this chapter and a validation of each WSDLC phases is achieved. The implementation shows that we were able to go through the process flow of the proposed schemes (QoWS management operations). These implementations are included also in our published papers [99], [100], [101], [102], and [103].

---

[1] The work presented in this chapter was published in [98], this work was extended to include also the lifecycle of a composite Web service and its implementation. This extension is expressed in section 4.3.3.

4.1 Introduction

As any software or component, developing Web services should follow a precise lifecycle. A lifecycle is a set of steps that guides Web services development process starting with requirement, then design, implementation, deployment, testing, and maintenance. Until now, there are no standard lifecycle models for Web services, neither from the developers view, nor from the users view. All proposals are still under experiment and need more improvement.

Since Web services architecture, protocols, tools, and technologies are expanding rapidly, WSDLC is becoming an important concern for Web services developers, Web services vendors, and Web services users. Web services developer will be supported in developing its Web services, as well as clients will be supported in discovering and using Web services. The objective is to define a model, or rather a methodology, to design, develop and maintain Web services; this is motivated by the limitations of existing WSDLC approaches ([29], [30], and [31]). The new WSDLC will define a process-oriented Web services model that captures activities such as publication, discovery, management, QoWS integration, QoWS verification, and QoWS composition. For each operation performed within the Web services model, a set of patterns should be defined to help in the achievement of each function. Semantic description of Web services lifecycle with its composition and interaction features should be addressed. The new WSDLC should include these design fundamentals in order to explore the potential benefits of Web services paradigm.

We will propose a new Web services development model to support the new requirements of Web services. We will include design features (patterns) while designing Web services in order to facilitate management and composition of Web services. We will also investigate in defining mechanisms to support QoS description, publication, and discovery of Web services and their QoWS.

The next section will survey the most important features of software and components development lifecycles.

4.2 Software Development Process vs. Component Development Process

Software Engineering development (respectively, Component-Based Development), as any other engineering discipline, has structured models for software development (respectively, Component-Based Development). In the following, we briefly describe the lifecycle of software and component development.

4.2.1 Software Development Lifecycle (SDLC)

The series of steps through which the software product progresses is called a lifecycle model [109]. Various lifecycle models are described in the literature; each of them has its strengths and weaknesses. Christiansson in [110] surveyed existing SDLCs and found that they have several commonalities and similar division of phases (also called processes). Table 1 shows these similarities in a general view of software system's lifecycle.

Table 1 General model of a software system's lifecycle

Phases	Short description of the purpose of each phase
Analysis	To understand the activities that software system is meant to support,
Design	To develop a detailed description of the software system,
Implementation	To formalize the design in an executable way,
Integration	To adjust the system to fit the existing software environment,
Test	To identify and eliminate the non desirable effects and errors and to verify the software system to satisfy all requirements,
Management	To keep the integrated software system up and running,
Administration	To perform follow-ups of the management and perform consecutive revisions of the integrated software system, and
Settlement	To settle the integrated software system (in part or as a whole) and to take charge of the information in the system.

4.2.2 Component Development Lifecycle (CDLC)

Various definitions for the term component have been suggested in the literature. One of these definitions is stated in [111] as *"A component is a software package which offers services through interfaces"*. Component development lifecycle is similar to the SDLC except in the implementation/acquisition phase, where the two lifecycles differ. Indeed, all over the design and development of a component, designers and/or developers make their decision to acquire the component from a software (component) vendor. This acquisition can be done either through purchase, outsourcing, in-house development, or component leasing. Lifecycle for component-based development can be seen from two perspectives: the client of the component and the developer or producer of the component. The component lifecycle from the producer perspective includes development, maintenance and retirement. However, the component lifecycle from the consumer perception starts with the acquisition of the component and then using it within a software system.

4.3 New WSDLC Proposal and Description of their Phases

To overcome the limitations stated in the related work on WSDLC presented in chapter 3, a structured Web services lifecycle model is needed. This model defines a process-oriented Web services model that considers Web services operations essentially publication, discovery, management, QoWS, and composition of Web services. For every operation performed within the Web services model, a set of patterns should be defined to help in the achievement of each function. Semantic description of Web service lifecycle with its composition and interaction features should be addressed. The new emerging Web services lifecycle should include these design fundamentals in order to explore the potential benefits of Web services paradigm.

Reusing existing software or component models might not be adequate for Web services for the following reasons:

- Not all phases of Web services development can be tackled in the same manner by existing SDLC or CDLC models. Differences are presented in some of the Web services phases described below. For example both the service provider and/or the service consumer could compose Web services together to create a composite Web service. Conversely, in SDLC the provider is the only one who has the ability to initiate the software composition.

- Most of the proposed lifecycle models don't support the description and the implementation of quality characteristics during their design, implementation, publication, and discovery phases.

- Because of the open nature of Web services and the multitudes of involved partners (Provider, Client, third party certifier), management of Web services is an important phase, which all phases in the Web services lifecycle should consider.

- Design phase is one of the essential phases in WSDLC. Modeling techniques should be explored to perform accurately this phase (e.g. UML, Method CASE of oracle). Existing lifecycles for Web services do not gain from the application of these modeling techniques to achieve the design phase.

4.3.1 WSDLC Overview of Basic Web Services

Most existing Web services engineering systems concentrate on the implementation phase and only few support the design phase [112]. The emergence of new Web services requires a defined requirements, specification, design and integration phases through a large-scale Web service lifecycle. WSDLC has to be decomposed into a set of phases that should take into consideration the open Web services environment and architecture, the multitude of technologies and protocols involved in this environment. Therefore we propose a WSDLC with phases that are more developed, and that support QoWS. These quality parameters are required for management, deployment and monitoring of Web services.

As described above (Figure 2), the proposed WSDLC consists of ten phases:

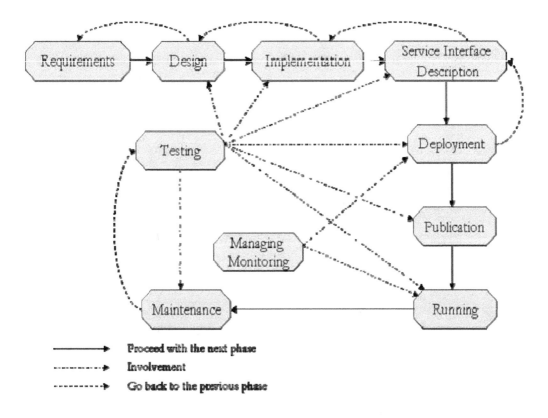

Figure 6 Web services lifecycle description

4.3.2 WSDLC Phases Description

4.3.2.1 Web Services Requirements

During this phase, analyses of functionalities a Web service is supposed to satisfy are defined. The Web services requirements consist of defining business constraints. From the Web services activities, requirements team members should decide whether some of them could be delegated to existing published Web services. The business process can be public and developers can reuse it as it is or adapt it for the development of new Web services. Also the Web service will be published, unlike other software. This will be the main differences between Web services requirement and software requirement. Requirements modeling for an example of a Multimedia Web service (MWS) we have developed for the sake of evaluating the proposed Lifecycle involve the activities listed below:

- Requirements capture and analysis: gathering information from MWS clients, evaluation of the client's application expectations, and determining how the client's of MWS will be served. The client's elicitation gathering can be done using requirements collection methodology (e.g. rapid prototyping, interviewing).

- Business process modeling and specification (selecting or creating an appropriate business process, use workflow to describe business process, reuse existing public business process and adjust it for a specific organization context). Modeling the video/audio streaming system requirements and writing the Web service requirements specification document.

- Constraints identification (Business constraints, Security constraints, etc).

- Requirements verification: verification of the MWS requirements in respect of client's elicitations and standards compliance. .

4.3.2.2 Web Services Design

The main goal of the design phase is to define how MWS Web services could be planned to provide the required functionalities while supporting the main quality attributes, such as manageability, security, and QoWS. The Web services design phase describes how the Web services should behave (expose its functionalities), and the Web service behavior may be described in several ways. However, the same Web service may behave in a different way to satisfy diverse client's requirements (e.g. gold, silver, bronze clients). The idea is to design different Web services interfaces that are able to provide sufficient information to the Web services users and environment. We strongly believe that information about Web service management, composition, QoWS, and other characteristics should be defined in the earlier phases of WSDLC, mainly in the design phase. Our approach is to divide Web services design into a set of sub-phases each one describes clearly the characteristics to be developed. For example design for manageability will describe manageability scope and functions. Moreover, it will expose a Web service as a manageable entity providing the following capabilities [113]: operations, events, interfaces, status, configuration, and metrics that can be used for managing and controlling Web services. Design for composition will describe Web services composition and their requirements. Design for QoWS will define QoWS prosperities their representation.

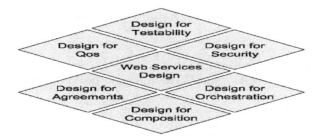

Figure 7 Design phase

Designing Web services and the quality parameters that attempt to support could be done using existing modeling languages like UML (Unified Modeling Language). The UML Profile for schedulability, performance and time is a recent Object Management Group (OMG) standard [114], which proposes a standard notation for performance and time modeling. The standard provides a set of stereotypes and tagged values to express a system's non-functional, time related characteristics. The stereotypes are used to annotate a model with information that is relevant for a particular situation for instance the period, work, worst-case execution time, and duration. Figure 8 presents an example of a sequence diagram of a MWS annotated with some QoWS attributes.

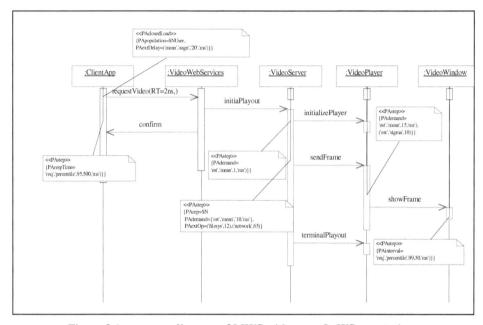

Figure 8 A sequence diagram of MWS with some QoWS annotations

4.3.2.3 Web Services Implementation

Web services implementation is the process of transforming the design in an executable way. Through this phase, Web services are implemented with respect to the main concepts described in the design phase and sub-phases. The same specification of Web services may be implemented in several different ways. Accordingly, we aim at insuring the integration of the performance parameters in the implementation of Web Services. During the implementation phase, developers need to choose the appropriate language, tools and protocols. A Web service should provide APIs to inform clients about operations such as move, copy, delete, and upgrade of the Web service. Implementing Web services can be performed in different ways:

- Implementing Web services from scratch: using existing Web services Toolkits (WSTK), such as BEA WebLogic [115]. Developers create a new Web service based on what has been designed in the design phase.

- Transforming applications into Web services: developers use available applications and work reversibly to define the operations that will be exposed as Web services, this operation is called wrapping. Using available WSTK, we generate Web services interface description using Web Services Description Language (WSDL). This interface defines how the functionality is to be accessed as a Web service.

- Composing new Web services from other Web services and applications: aggregation of multiple Web services and applications to compose a single Web service is another way to develop Web services. Composite Web services can be built, either statically or dynamically. In static composition, the "composition logic" is known in advance. In dynamic composition, the "composition logic" is determined in real time relying on service discovery techniques. A detailed description of lifecycle of composite Web services is proposed in section 4.3.3.

- Web service source code acquisition: this can be performed by acquiring source code from vendors or downloading free open source code, adapting it and exposing it as Web services via interface description.

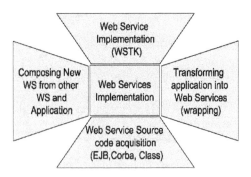

Figure 9 Web services implementation

4.3.2.4 Creation or Generation of Web Services Interface Description

Once the implementation phase is completed, the Web service interface description can be developed or generated using the existing Web services development tools (e.g. IBM WSTK, BEA WebLogic [115]). The Web service interface is described using WSDL. A Web service interface should show the published operations of the Web service as well as translating guidelines defined in the design phase. Web services Implementation Description (WSID) describes how functionalities are to be exposed as a Web service and how to invoke the service functionalities. The WSDL document created or generated during this phase contains also the description of the service implementation, which is based on how and where the service is deployed i.e. the network location where the service is deployed.

The service implementation has several distinct interfaces that provide different Web services functions. This simplifies the way in which a particular requester (manager, security agent, etc.) uses a Web service. Upgrading Web services by adding new functions should give the possibility to upgrade these interfaces and/or create a new category of interfaces.

Figure 10 displays possible Web service interfaces created to expose Web service functionalities to its requester. These interfaces fulfill different purposes, and provide

72

different types of information: manageability, composition, and QoWS information. The number of interfaces by a given Web service depends on the nature of this Web service and its desired requesters. For example, in Figure 10, Web service 4 has two interfaces. It is a simple Web service supplying a single unique function and doesn't compose other services. Conversely, Web service 1 is a more complex Web service that supports multiple different interfaces, for manageability, composition, etc. Because of the demanding nature of some users of that Web service, and the multitude of functions that it offers, or its participation in a composition of other services, this service has to be continuously available, secure, and manageable.

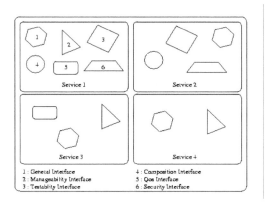

Figure 10 Interfaces Description phase

4.3.2.5 Web Service Deployment

The executable code of a Web service has to be deployed in a run-time environment, i.e. a hosting platform. This phase is also concerned with the configuration of the application server running on this platform with all technologies needed to invoke the service (handling SOAP requests, XML parsing, etc.) and perform its functionality (e.g. access to needed databases or other Web services). After the deployment phase, the service is ready to be used by a service requester.

4.3.2.6 Publication of Web Service Interface

A group from Cardiff University has developed UDDIe [71] registry as an extension to the known standards UDDI. UDDIe supports the notion of "blue pages", to record user defined properties associated with a service, and to enable the discovery of services based on these published proprieties. Searching for quality attributes of a Web service is achieved by extending the businessService class in UDDI with propertyBag, and the "find" method to enable queries to UDDI to be based on numeric and logical (AND/OR) ranges. UDDIe can co-exist with existing UDDI and enable a query to be issued to both simultaneously. UDDIe has been implemented as open source software. Table 2 illustrates the interface description of an example of a MWS we have developed to validate our Lifecycle. The description includes also the specification of the QoWS the MWS service is providing.

Table 2 WSDL description of Multimedia Web service and its QoS

```
<?xml version="1.0" encoding="UTF-8"?>
<wsdl:definitions
.....
 <wsdl:message name="getVideoResponse">
   <wsdl:part name="return" type="SOAP-ENC:string"/>
 </wsdl:message>
....
 <wsdl:portType name="VideoService">
   <wsdl:operation name=" getVideoClasses " parameterOrder="symbol">
     <wsdl:input message="intf:getVideoClassRequest"/>
     <wsdl:output message="intf:getVideoClassResponse"/>
   </wsdl:operation>
 </wsdl:portType>
......
<wsdl:binding name=" VideoWSSoap" type="intf:VideoService">
   <wsdlsoap:binding style="rpc"
....                              ┌─────────────────┐
 </wsdl:binding>                  │ Differentiated  │
<wsdl:QoS serviceClass="1">       │ class of QoWS   │
        <cpu_count>100</cpu_count>└─────────────────┘
        <disk_storage>150</disk_storage>
        <Capacity>1000 <Capacity/>      ┌──────────────┐
</wsdl:QoS>                             │ Guaranteed QoS│
<wsdl:QoS serviceClass="2">             │ per service  │
   <Service operationName="getLastPrice" ResponseTime="5"/> resources
   <Service operationName="getPeriod" ResponseTime="10"/>
</wsdl:QoS>                      ┌──────────────┐
.....                           │ Guaranteed QoS│
</wsdl:definitions>             │ per operation │
                                └──────────────┘
```

The Web services Interface description once created has to be published into a service registry. The Web services clients can requests the UDDIe registry and specify the QoS requirement within its request. Table 3 shows a client request augmented with QoS requirement to the UDDIe registry.

75

Table 3 Client request to UDDIe with specified QoS

```
<find_service generic="2.0" xmlns="urn:uddi-org:api_v2">
<name>MathService</name>
<propertylBag>
<property>
<propertyFindQualifier>equal_to</propertyFindQualifier>
        <propertyName>cpu_count</propertyName>
        <propertyType>number</propertyType>
        <propertyValue>100</propertyValue>
</property>
<property>
<propertyFindQualifier>equal_to</propertyFindQualifier>

        <propertyName>disk_storage</propertyName>
        <propertyType>number</propertyType>
        <propertyValue>150</propertyValue>
</property>
</propertyBag>
</find_service>
```

4.3.2.7 Running Web Services

During the run phase, Web services are fully available for invocation. At this point, they are fully deployed, operational and accessible at the service provider. Running composite Web services is more complicated because it requires selecting at runtime Web services that have to satisfy requirement of the composition. Also, orchestrating interaction between all partners within a runtime environment is required. In addition, a dynamic adaptation of composition needs to be initiated to accommodate possible changes (adding new services, deleting or replacing services, etc.).

4.3.2.8 Managing and Monitoring Web Services

A managed Web service describes very often a managed resource and exposes a set of management interfaces. Through the management interfaces, the underlying resources can be managed and controlled. Management of Web services covers many aspects, such as Web service's instances management, billing management, access management, composition management, fault management, etc.

Management phase (see Figure 6) is involved in most of the lifecycle phases and plays an important role all through the development process.

4.3.2.9 Testing Web Services

Testing procedures can be applied in all of WSDLC stages. Particularly; it is performed through the design phase to verify consistency and correctness of the design. In the implementation phase, testing denotes the identification and elimination of non-desirable effects and errors, and also verifies if requirements are satisfied. This should include tasks such as service integration and deployment testing. Web services are tested based on their cooperation (dynamic behavior) in addition to their individual functionalities. Testing composite Web services consists of verifying the interactions between composing Web services using a flow model or a global model, and validates the correctness of the composition structure.

Web services interfaces need to be tested after their creation or generation. Testing a Web service interface consists of verifying the correctness of WSDL document and its association with service implementation (test if the methods exposed via the Web services interface is responding and returning the expected results). Testing is also present in Web services deployment phase. Its goal is to verify and test the Web services platform, protocols and tools to adjust Web services to their specific environment. Other testing actions have to be applied at the Web services running phase, testing process during this phase is very hard to accomplish. Dynamic are Web services and automated testing using tools will be a good approach to perform testing Web services at runtime.

4.3.2.10 Web Services Maintenance

Maintenance in WSDLC is an important process involved in several phases all through the development of Web services lifecycle. Maintenance phase includes correction of bugs that were not detected during the test phase (corrective maintenance). It includes also upgrading and adapting of Web services to changing client requirements (enhancement maintenance). After enhancing Web services functionalities, the provider has to insure that the previous published Service interface is still assured (regression testing). Replacement of Web services with services that offer the same functionality is performed during the maintenance phase when services are not operating and adaptive maintenance is not possible. The maintenance phase is a very crucial and costly phase in Web services engineering. However, it is not covered in most of existing WSDLCs. Web services retirement is a maintenance action and leads to a Web services replacement or to end providing a Web service.

The next section will present the QoWS properties description of Web services and an example of differentiated classes of a Web service driven QoWS.

4.3.3 QoWS Properties Annotations and Classification

In this section, we classify some QoWS properties, and we assessed their usefulness for evaluating the performance of Web services.

4.3.3.1 QoWS Parameters for Web Services

A Web service can be selected based on the quality characteristics exposed to the clients (e.g., is it available enough? fast enough? and expected to answer requests on an acceptable time?). During service invocation, the values of QoWS metrics need to be monitored and checked against predefined and expected values. When deviations are detected, dynamic adaptation mechanisms need to be triggered. QoWS represents the non-functional aspects of the service being provided to the Web service users. A wide variety of QoWS parameters have been presented in pervious work ([35], [36], [37], [38], [39], [116]). In our work, we will consider the following QoWS attributes:

Response time (RT): the time a service takes to respond to the client request. This attribute is measured at the client side, it can also be measured at the server side and it has to be monitored to measure the time the request (send/receive) spends in transiting the network. This metric represents the difference between the time of sending the request and the time of receiving an answer. Response time value includes the round-trip communication and the processing delays in servicing the client request ([37], [38], [39], and [116]).

Service charge: the cost involved in requesting the service. The Web service cost can be estimated by operation or by volume of data.

Availability: the probability that the service is accessible (available for use) [116] or the percentage of time that the service is operating [39]. To compute this parameter we observe the service during a period of time and we measure the availability as the percentage of uptime of a service during this observation period. A long period of observation gives a more accurate approximation for the service availability.

Processing Time: the time between the arrival of a service request and the time the corresponding response is generated [38]. This metric is computed at the provider side.

Reputation: measure of service trustworthiness. It depends on end users' experiences of using the service. Different users may have different opinions on the same service. The reputation value is given by the average ranking given to the service by several users [39]. For example, in Amazon.com and eBay, the range is [0,5].

A detailed QoWS classification model of Web services is provided in appendix A.

4.3.3.2 Differentiated Classes of a Web Service

Selecting suitable Web services regarding the QoWS provision is a determinant factor to ensure customer satisfaction. Different users may have different requirements and preferences regarding QoWS. For example, a user may require minimizing the response time (RT) while satisfying certain constraints in terms of price and reputation; while another user may give more importance to the price than to the response time. A QoWS classification is therefore needed to describe different QoWS requirements for various user profiles. Each class of service corresponds to a specific level of quality of service. Since WSDL is XML-based, it is possible to describe multiple levels of QoWS the provider can provide within the same WSDL document.

Different classes of service may be considered, either depending on a classification of users in occasional buyers, regular clients and VIP clients, or depending on a service charge which the user is willing to pay. It is therefore appropriate to provide different classes of services, not only in terms of available options, but also in terms of QoWS, especially services availability and response time.

To illustrate this, clients can be classified of being platinum clients, gold clients, or silver clients. For every class of QoWS, a related category of client is selected. Each class is described by a set of QoWS attributes a Web service can offer. It exposes different QoWS attributes with different values. These attributes include response time, availability, processing time, reputation, and service charge. Table 4 describes an example of QoWS classes according to a set of QoWS attributes.

Table 4 Differentiated classes of a Web service

Class of Web service / QoWS Parameters	Class 1	Class 2	Class 3	...	Class n
Response Time	N/A	0.7 ms	0.5 ms		0.1ms
Processing Time	N/A	N/A	0.1 ms		0.01 ms
Availability	N/A	N/A	0.8		1 (100%)
Reputation	N/A	N/A	N/A		5/5
Service charge	0.10 $	0.2 $	0.25$		0.35$

N/A: not applicable.

The QoWS metrics shown in Table 4 are chosen because they reflect what most users are expecting from Web services in term of performance support. In addition, they are useful criteria for evaluating the performance of Web services. Each of these QoWS attributes is calculated using computation logic and is either static or measured at runtime. These QoWS metrics can be measured at the client or the provider side or via a third party entity (e.g. Broker). If the QoWS measurement is delegated to a third party, it should acquire the authorization and the required capabilities from the client and the provider. Moreover, the time consumed by this third party to handle delegated operations will be reflected in the measured QoWS properties (e.g. response time).

4.4 WSDLC Overview of a Composite Web Service

Composition of Web services is the process of aggregating a set of Web services to create a more complete Web service with a wide range of functionalities. Aggregating Web services together have to be according to a set of design principals and following a set of phases. We strongly believe that Web services composition is a separate lifecycle since it is a dynamic and complex process that shows new requirements comparing to the lifecycle of a basic Web services. Figure 11 presents a proposition of lifecycle for composite Web services with consideration of QoWS management.

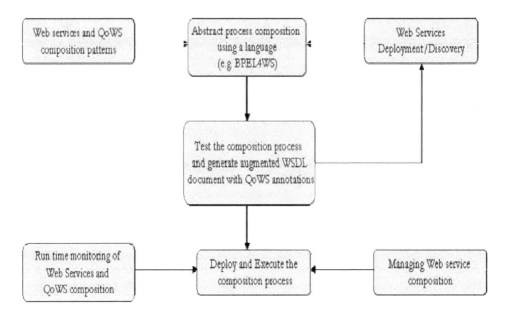

Figure 11 Composite Web services lifecycle

As described in Figure 11 a composite Web services lifecycle involves a set of steps as shown in the above figure. A description of each of these step and their contribution to whole lifecycle are presented below.

Web services discovery: is the operation that allows the discovery and the localization of Web services that will participate in the composition process. The discovery provides the requestor with the service description that holds the information about the service location. The requestor (abstract process composition) uses this information to bind to the service and invoke their operations.

Abstract process composition: is a formal definition of the composition process which identifies the services partners in a given composition, the specification and the orchestration of their interactions, the sequences of planned activities, and the generation of interface description of the composite Web service.

Web Services and QoWS composition patterns: are a set of design principles that can be applied while composing Web services and also their offered QoWS. These patterns are defined according to the way Web services partners are invoked and derived from the composition process. A detailed description of these composition patterns will be presented in more details in chapter 6.

Test the composition process: this will enable the testing (static testing) of the composition process at the design phase. It consists of the verification of BPEL document and applying Web services composition patterns and also the QoWS composition patterns. The result of this phase leads to the extension of a WSDL interface of a composite Web services with the QoWS annotations.

Deploy and execute the composition process: at this phase, Web services partners have to be fully deployed, and available for the composition process. It consists of executing the composite service specifications while satisfying quality constraints, e.g. availability, response time, cost, and other properties.

Monitoring executed Web services composition: it consists of a continuous observation of Web services in addition to their QoWS. A concise monitoring of composite Web service and their QoWS requires the monitoring of all the set of Web services partners and their QoWS. The monitoring procedures can be divided into different directions according to the expected monitoring goals. Therefore, we can distinguish between monitoring for fault detection, monitoring QoWS, etc.

Managing Web services composition: the management is based either on the feedbacks received from monitoring operations and/or the organizational changes regarding the new emerging technologies. Adaptation mechanisms can be tackled to manage the Web service composition or a complete new Re-composition can be applied.

The evaluation of the lifecycle of composite Web services presented above is performed in chapter 6, where architecture for QoS composition, validation, and monitoring was proposed. Most of the phases are respected and management operations were implemented.

4.5 WSDLCs Key Benefits

Our model offers various benefits to Web service developers. In the following, we highlight the advantages of our proposed WSDLCs for both basic and composite Web services over existing models.

- It facilitates monitoring and controlling of Web services: monitor and control a Web service during its lifecycle require available information provided by the management interface of the Web service. Other features of management are developed in the Web service itself (e.g. reporting on the Web service state: active, responding, not responding, etc.). Monitoring composite Web services and their QoWS is more complex than monitoring a basic Web service, this is due to the distributed context and the multitude of Web services participants.

- The proposed WSDLCs support the description and the publication of valuable information about Web services QoWS, management, and security. This information is structured and accessible via Web services interfaces (e.g. version history, priority, relationships, constraints, etc.). Value added Web services attributes are described in WSDL document and published through UDDIe registry.

- The adoption of WSDLCs might reduce design, development, and deployment complexity: The creation of different interfaces for Web service makes Web services flexible, easy to extend and maintain. The presence of maintenance phase will also help to reduce complexity through enhancement of each phase with new features.

- WSDLCs introduces maintenance of Web services during and after its development, which will reduce Web services development cost. Maintenance phase is a very important and costly phase in Web services development process.

- Investigate on Web services design during WSDLC will pay off throughout service maintenance, once the service has to be adapted and modified.

- Implementation of Web services with respect to its WSDLCs includes knowledge of finding, copying, moving, and deleting Web services. This information will be defined in Web service implementation and will be accessed through management interfaces (e.g. when service moves from location to a new location, it notifies all connected services). This service will publish the new version of WSDL and will update its Web service description implementation. The new WSDL document will include the old one and will be available for future clients through UDDI registry.

- WSDLCs speed up the design, development, deployment, management and control of Web services. This will reduce Web services development cost.

- Support classes of QoWS and their composition for composite Web services. Most of the existing solutions are use one category of QoWS for different classes of clients. However, clients may have different and continuously changing QoWS requirements. None of the approaches consider the composition of classes of QoWS.

- Test and validate the composition of Web services with the QoWS it supports to both clients and providers before and after selecting a composite Web service. A WSDL document of composite Web services is augmented with QoWS annotations.

4.6 Summary

Since Web services architecture, protocols, tools, and technologies are expanding rapidly, WSDLC is becoming an important concern for Web service engineering. An important need for a general model to be used for designing, developing and maintaining Web services was our principal motivation.

In this chapter, we proposed WSDLC for both basic and composite Web services. We have chosen to divide WSDLC to a set of phases to be followed during the development of Web services. All along this decomposition, we gave more consideration to the design and implementation phases. Design phase was decomposed into sub-phases called points of concern. Each phase defines and provides design solution to a specific sub-characteristic (QoS, management, etc.). These characteristics are strongly correlated. We have also investigated how the activities of service management, deployment, and implementation can benefit from the availability of an explicit design representation that is enhanced with management capabilities. Through the implementation phase, the concepts defined in the design phase are correctly coded and service interfaces are developed.

Chapter 5

Broker-Based Architecture for QoWS Management of Basic Web Services (QBA-WS)

5.1 Introduction

The initial specifications of Web services, regarding functional and interfacing aspects, deal with the issues of service publication and service discovery but not with the issue of Web service selection, and QoWS management. Service discovery, handled by UDDI and WSDL, copes with finding Web service implementations that meet a particular service description and particular requirements such as the cost of service delivery and QoWS requirements.

Service selection copes with choosing a Web service, among those discovered for the given description, to handle customer requests. It is the main problem given that discovery alone is not sufficient to find the most appropriate Web services that can deliver the required QoWS. Indeed, the discovery of Web services will be based not only on the functional requirements (i.e., the case of existing approaches) but also on the QoWS requirements of the service. One of the key differentiators between Web services providers offering the same web service will be the levels of QoWS they can support. In addition to service selection, the support of QoWS involves a number of QoWS management functions, such as QoWS verification and certification, QoWS negotiation, and QoWS monitoring.

QoWS verification and certification enable providers to evaluate their services as well as the level of QoWS they can provide prior to the publication of their Web services. Negotiation mechanisms allow reaching an agreed upon QoWS between the user and the

87

provider. Monitoring mechanisms allow the notification of users and providers when their agreed upon QoWS is violated. Adaptation mechanisms maintain the agreed upon QoWS in response to QoWS violation.

For the above reasons, a need for a novel architecture for QoWS management and assurance is very urgent. This architecture has to provide support for QoWS-driven Web services selection, QoWS specification, QoWS verification and certification, QoWS publication, QoWS discovery, QoWS monitoring, and QoWS negotiation between clients and potential providers. These QoWS management operations should be supported without disturbing the overall Web services environment, with reasonable cost, and minimal overhead at both provider's and client's environments.

This chapter presents a QoWS broker-based architecture for QoWS support in Web services environments. Among the important goals of the architecture is the support of clients in selecting Web services based on specific required QoWS. To achieve this goal, we propose a two-phase verification and certification technique that is performed by a third party broker. The first phase consists of verifying the service interface description including the QoWS parameters description. The second phase consists of applying a measurement technique to compute the QoWS metrics stated in the service interface and compares their values with the claimed ones. This is used to verify the conformity of a Web service to its description from a QoWS point of view (QoWS testing). Therefore, a set of QoWS test cases have been defined and used as input to QoWS verification. The configuration and generation of these test cases is described in more details in chapter 7. Once the Web service passes the verification tests, the broker issues a conformance certificate to certify that QoWS claims are valid. A QoWS negotiation based algorithm is then proposed to allow negotiating QoWS classes between providers and clients of Web services.

We also introduce, in this chapter, a measurement driven QoWS monitoring scheme to monitor, at runtime, the QoWS such as response time, processing time, and availability. We have implemented a prototype of our architecture that includes the verifier, certifier, negotiator, and the monitor components of the broker. We have performed some experiments to evaluate the importance of verification and certification features in the selection process using real Web services. The details about the implementation of our architecture are described in chapter 7. We published the work presented in this chapter in the following conferences ([99], [100], [101], [102], and [103]).

We developed a prototype of our QBA-WS architecture which includes all the involved entities (e.g. Broker, etc.). Also, we evaluate empirically each QoWS management operation.

In our proposed architecture, for the sake of better QoWS support and management, we have integrated two main approaches for QoWS management that we describe in section 3.5.2. Our architecture is based on an independent brokerage entity that will be used to verify, certify, and monitor QoWS. Also, we have proposed an extension to existing Web services protocols to support QoWS description, publication and discovery. The adopted solution offers the following benefits:

(1) It shields the application of the provider and the client from the complexity of QoWS management;

(2) It benefits from the adoption of extension to the Web services protocols stack mainly WSDL, UDDI, and SOAP to support QoWS management operations;

(3) It allows providers to extend the service description with QoWS-centered annotations;

(4) It allows clients to express their required services with QoWS requirements;

(5) It includes a validation process that enables providers to test their service interface as well as the level of QoWS they can provide, prior to publishing the service;

(6) It supports client during Web service selection based on client requirement and QoWS verification and certification;

(7) It makes the broker component transparent and available to all concerned parties including the Web service provider and the requestor since the architecture is based on Web services;

(8) It upgrades regularly the information stored in the broker database to cope with the continuous occurred changes related to the Web service description;

(9) It provides support for QoWS negotiation between clients and providers;

(10) It allows monitoring of the agreed QoWS between clients and providers and, therefore, it detects any QoWS violation.

5.2 Requirements and Assumptions

The architecture presented below supposes that the Web service, since it is a QoS-aware Web service, should support an admission control mechanism. Admission control is the process of discriminating which request is admitted to use a Web service. In other words, it is the way of controlling what type of requests is allowed to access the Web service. The type of requests differs from simple requests to more complex requests those soliciting a specific level of QoWS. Admission control schemes need to be implemented at the Web service side (application server) to control the client's requests entering to the Web service. A client application that wishes to use operations offered by a given Web service specifies the required level of QoWS it is looking for. The Web service judges whether this specific request is allowed to invoke its operation with the requested level of QoWS. Then, it may accept or reject the received request. The admission control scheme is often achieved using an admission manager component that applies a policy driven algorithm to admit or reject request according to predefined policies.

Many initiatives were proposed in the literature to implement an admission control mechanism within the provider infrastructure ([104], [105], [106], [107], and [108]). Most of these mechanisms implement at least the following operations:

1. acceptation and classification of incoming requests from customers,

2. maintaining a state information base (SIB) about resources, services levels of QoS advertised by Web Services, and the maximum capacity of each server to support each class of QoWS,

3. verification if the client's requests are allowed to use the specific class of QoWS,

4. determination of the set of QoS-aware Web Services able to deliver the customer required service based on the published QoS and the QoS requested by the customer,

5. selection of suitable target server able to satisfy the customer required QoS according to some selection policy implemented by the admission manager,

6. notification of customers of the approval or rejection of their requests, and

7. gathering of runtime information about the current state of servers in terms of availability, load, and the level of QoWS the service can deliver.

5.3 QBA-WS: Components and Interfaces

5.3.1 Architecture Description

The architecture extends the standard Service Oriented Architecture (SOA) with QoWS support for Web services. It includes QoWS description during the service publication, and performs invocation of Web services based on their QoWS. In addition, it verifies, certifies, negotiates, and monitors QoWS dynamically using a Web service broker. The architecture adds to the SOA a third party Web service Broker and substitutes the normal UDDI registry by a QoWS-enabled UDDIe registry. Also, it involves the other two main participating roles that are the Web service provider, and the Web service client. Components of the architecture are presented in Figure 12. A sequence of typical interactions between these components is presented in Figure 13.

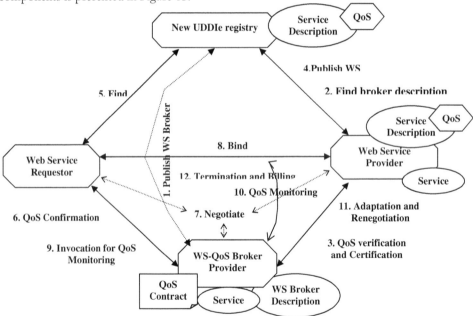

Figure 12 A QoWS broker-based architecture

The broker publishes its interface description in the UDDIe registry (operation 1 in Figure 12). The Web services provider looks for the broker's WSDL document in the UDDIe registry (operation 2). Then, it requests the broker to certify the conformity of Web services to its description including the claimed QoWS (operation 3). The Web services provider publishes its QoS-aware Web services in the UDDIe registry (operation 4). Clients can check the UDDIe registry for QoS-enabled Web services satisfying their needs (operation 5). Before starting the negotiation process with the provider, clients have the possibility to confirm that the published classes of QoWS have been previously certified by the broker (operation 6). The broker arbitrates the QoWS negotiation between the client and the provider (operation 7). If an agreement is reached, the client binds to the Web service using the agreed class of QoWS (operation 8). During invocation, the client can ask the broker to monitor and control the delivered QoWS (operation 9 and 10). If the QoWS degrades, the broker notifies the provider (the provider has an interface to get back QoWS notification) which initiates QoWS adaptation in order to maintain the agreed QoWS (operation 11). The QoWS renegotiation is initiated if the adaptation operations fail to maintain the agreed QoWS (operation 11). The QoWS management processes terminate by releasing resources and issuing the corresponding bill (operation 12).

Figure 12 presents a broker-based architecture with features that overcome the limitations of existing approaches, described in the literature review of chapter 3. Its important features include the support of service selection based on client QoWS requirements, QoWS verification and certification. QoWS verification is the process of validating the correctness of information described in the service interface including QoWS parameters. The QoWS verification is performed using an approach that builds test cases to measure QoWS parameters. The verification is used as input for the certification: once the verification succeeds a certificate is issued. The broker guides the negotiation process between clients and their providers until they reach an agreement. The negotiation is based on the QoWS classes and guided by a negotiation algorithm executed by both clients and providers. During Web service invocation, the broker measures QoWS attributes and uses their values to monitor the provision of the selected QoWS level; it notifies the interested entities of any QoWS violation. The broker updates, regularly, its database whenever significant changes happen. In the architecture, the certification process goes beyond certifying just the QoWS provider's claims. Additional tests can be performed to make sure that these QoWS claims are fulfilled.

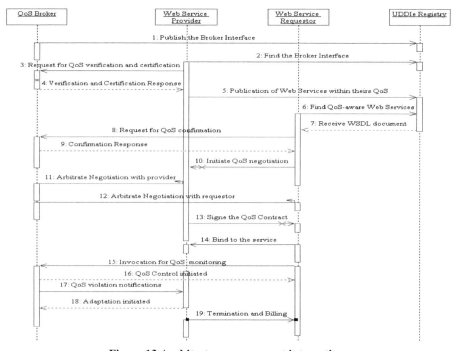

Figure 13 Architecture component interactions

Web Services Broker: The broker is a Web service or set of Web services that assist clients in selecting Web services based on a set of QoWS parameters. It is responsible for conducting a collection of QoWS related management operation such as verification and certification, negotiation, monitoring, and adaptation.

Web services Provider: The provider is the entity that develops the Web service and describes its functionalities in addition to the QoWS it provides. One of the important duties of the provider is to invoke the broker to verify its QoS-aware Web services. The provider is also involved in the QoWS negotiation, monitoring, and adaptation.

Web services client: The client application operates as a service consumer of the advertised Web services. The most important operation performed by the client is selecting Web services that meet a requested QoWS. This operation is based on the verification and certification of QoWS performed by the broker.

UDDI Enabled QoS Registry: UDDIe is a registry that supports QoWS publication and discovery [98]. The UDDIe registry has been developed in Cardiff University as an extension to the standard UDDI registry. UDDIe supports the notion of "blue pages", to record user defined properties associated with a Web service, and to enable the discovery of services based on these.

5.4 Broker Design

The QoWS broker consists of the following components: Admission manager, User profile manager, QoWS negotiator, Selection manager, QoWS monitor, QoWS verifier/certifier, QoWS information manager, and a database. The components of the broker, presented in Figure 14 and which are enclosed by a dashed line, concern both provider and client while the verifier/certifier component concerns only the provider of Web services.

95

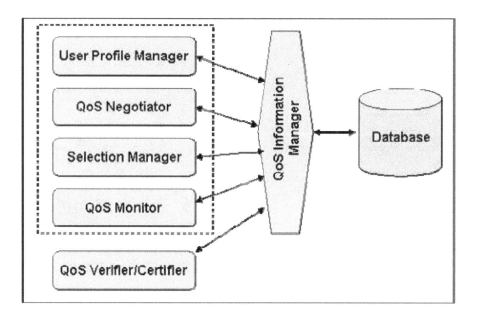

Figure 14 QoS Broker Design

QoWS Information Manager: The *QoWS information manager* is in charge of specifying the QoS parameters of interest according to the users required QoWS, and collecting actual values for these parameters from the Web services providers. QoWS information as well as information regarding QoWS violations is maintained in the broker's database. The other components of the broker get QoWS information from the QoWS Information manager to achieve their objectives. This information might be useful for services providers to enhance their QoS-aware Web services.

User Profile Manager: The *User Profile Manager* is responsible for managing users' preferences and their required QoWS. This allows the user to update its preferences and required QoWS after receiving, for example, a certain level of QoWS.

QoWS negotiator: The *QoWS negotiator* is in charge of conducting and managing the negotiation process through a negotiation protocol. At the end of the negotiation and after an agreement is reached, the QoWS negotiator defines and issues the clauses of the QoWS contract, which specifies what the provider should deliver, the guaranteed QoWS, and the cost. The contract is stored in the broker's database, and a copy of it is sent to both the user and the provider. A detailed negotiation process is presented in section 5.6.

Selection Manager: the *Selection Manager* is in charge of implementing different selection policies in order to provide an acceptable quality of service to the users. These policies can range from simple policies, as random and round robin, to complex ones taking into account the current state of servers in terms of availability, load, and level of quality of service they can deliver.

QoWS Monitor: The *QoWS Monitor* is responsible for monitoring the QoWS that is being delivered by Web services providers to clients. The monitoring process is based on the information described in the contract stored in the broker's database. A detailed description of this process is described in section 5.7.

QoWS verifier and Certifier: The *QoWS Verifier* is responsible for verifying Web services and their QoS. The verification is performed based on information received from providers and the results of the tests performed by the broker. This information concerns Web services location (URL), and QoWS information description. The QoWS verifier performs the following tasks:

- It asks for information about the provider and its Web service (Servers' resources capacity, connections used, Network information, etc.).

- It checks the WSDL files of the Web services under consideration (location, interface and implementation description)

- It checks the correctness of the information provided by the services providers.

- It makes sure that all published operations are available.

- It verifies the QoWS described in WSDL. The QoWS verifier can initiate, if necessary, additional tests to validate other information provided in the WSDL document. This information concerns QoWS attributes classification (definition, computation logic, upper and lower bounds).

- It stores the verification report in the broker database.

Databases: The broker's *database* stores information generated by the broker's components: User profile manager, QoWS verifier/certifier, QoWS negotiator, QoWS monitor, and QoWS information manager. It also supplies information to these components. Information stored in the database comprises certificates, verification and confirmation reports, monitoring information, etc.

5.5 Application Support for QoWS Publication and Discovery

To guide both the clients and providers of Web services in the discovery and the publication of Web services using the UDDIe registry, we have developed an application that supports these operations (Figure 15, Figure 16). This application:

- supports providers during the publication process, and validates the description of QoWS defined in the WSDL document by offering providers with the possibility to parse the WSDL document and display a list of its QoWS properties. They can then add, update, and/or remove some QoWS records from the list. When they run the publication process, the WSDL document will be updated automatically.

- allows Web services' clients to append in their requests the QoS properties they are looking for during the discovery process of Web services.

- allows easier and more flexible interactions with the UDDIe for both clients and providers.

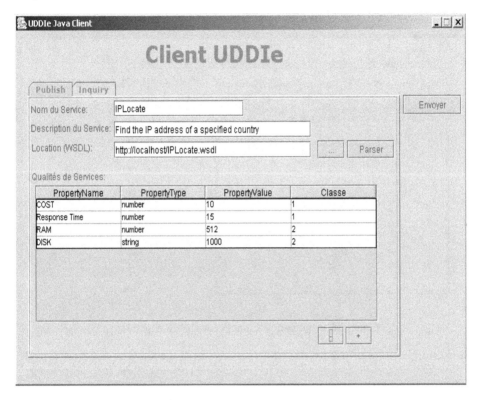

Figure 15 Application support for QoS publication

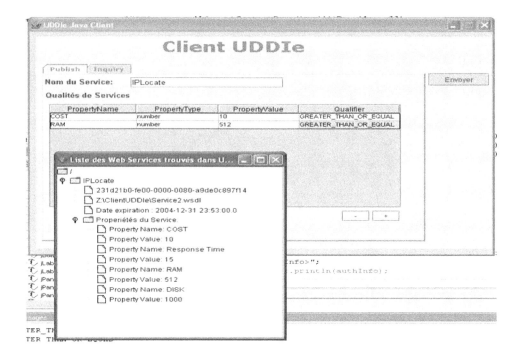

Figure 16 Application support for QoWS discovery

Publication: In order to publish their Web services using the above application, providers should supply the service name, description, and the location of WSDL document (Figure 15). Through the application interface, the provider uploads the service description (WSDL document), which is parsed to validate its content and to display the list of QoWS classes including attributes' names, types, and values. The Web service description document uses additional XML tags to describe QoWS classes in terms of QoWS attributes and their related values (Table 4). The validation process of the WSDL document verifies the correctness of its published operations in addition to the QoWS information. Using the application interface, the Web service provider can add and remove QoWS attributes to/from its service description before going through the publication process. The WSDL document is then

100

updated accordingly. At this stage, the WSDL document is validated and the provider publishes the QoS-enabled Web service interface description.

Discovery: this operation is available to Web service clients to guide them in the process of selecting Web services with QoS requirements (Figure 16). A client queries the registry and specifies the service name (optional) and the set of required QoS attributes and their related values (e.g. look for IP_Locator Web services, that returns the location of a given IP address; a client can specify conditions such as: cost less than $25 and response time less than 20 ns). The client has the possibility to fully edit the query before issuing it. A list of Web services' descriptions that fulfill the client's requirements is displayed via the application interface. The frame contains the list of QoWS classes with their corresponding values, as well as the Web service definition.

An added value of this application is that it invokes the verifier component which is described in the next section to validate and verify the WSDL documents and their QoWS. It also generates the client's request that specifies QoWS requirements which is submitted then to the UDDIe. The result of this query is a detailed description of suitable Web service and their QoWS. This will significantly help the client to make a decision and select the Web service that best meets his/her needs.

The next section describes in depth the model used to verify and certify QoWS stated in this section.

5.6 QoWS Broker Verification and Certification Model

QoWS verification and certification are two main functions that the proposed QoWS broker supports in addition to other QoWS management functions. They can be considered as keys differentiators of the proposed broker compared to existing approaches ([38], [53], [77], [78], [79]). Web services providers request the QoWS broker for QoWS certification before publishing their WSDL with QoWS classes in UDDIe registry. Before issuing a conformance certificate, the Web service should pass a list of verification tests. In the following subsections, we describe the verification and certification functions and show how they are used to improve the utilization of Web services.

5.6.1 Verification Scenarios

The verification process is initiated by the service provider through the "invokeBroker" operation of the Web service verifier. During the invocation, the Web service provider supplies the verifier with its WSDL document and additional information about resources available within the provider (operation 1 in Figure 17). Then, the verifier sends this document to the WSDL parser. We have implemented a parser application that extracts all useful information from the WSDL document including the QoS properties (operation 2) and stores them in the broker database (operation 3). This information includes the service name, the location, the implementation description, the QoWS properties names, types and values. The next operation performed by the service verifier is to test the service URI, the XML schema definition, the service binding information, and the availability of all operations described in the service interface (operation 4). The service verifier checks also if all the operations described in the service interface are available by invoking these operations using the client application of the verifier.

The verifier goes beyond the above verification functions and performs as well the verification of the QoWS information introduced in the service interface. QoWS verification is conducted through a set of test cases executed by the service verifier to verify the conformity of QoWS properties claimed by a provider. To perform each test case, the verifier asks for additional information about the provider and its Web service (Server capacity, Network bandwidth, etc.). QoWS verification process is detailed in the implementation section and includes the verification of Response Time, Availability, and the Price properties. In addition, more details about test cases selection, deployment, and execution are described in the implementation chapter (chapter 7).

Once the verification operation is terminated the verifier stores the verification result in its database (operation 5). It uses the stored information to produce a verification report as shown in Figure 18 (operation 6). The service provider has the access to its verification reports via a Web site using a username/password authentication policy (operation 7).

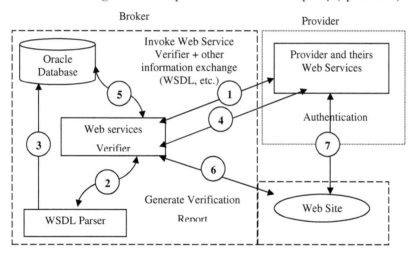

Figure 17 Verification scenarios

The verification process deals with three verification levels (see Figure 18) that are: general Web services information validation, WSDL document content validation, and QoWS description validation. A Web service is said to be compliant with a given level when it passes the corresponding set(s) of tests described in the verification document.

Based on this document, the Web service is classified for example into one of the followings: Silver Web services, Bronze Web services, and Gold Web services. A Bronze Web service is, for instance, a Web service for which most of the verification scenarios failed. A Silver Web service is a service for which more than 80% of verification tests succeeded. A Web service is qualified as Gold if all the verification tests succeeded. Figure 18 outlines an example of a Tri_Stat Web service and its compliance to some level of verification criteria. Tri_Stat is a Web service that we developed for testing purposes. Tri_Stat Web service provides a set of statistics and math functions (e.g. Poisson, Median, etc.) and implements some data sorting algorithm (e.g. quick sort, shell sort, etc.). The Tri_Stat describes and supports also the provision of a set of QoWS metrics defined in section 5.2.2.1

Figure 18 Verification report for Tri_Stat Web services

5.6.2 QoWS Conformity Certification

Once the verification is passed successfully, the certification process is initiated. The certification process consists of issuing a certificate to the service provider. This certificate states that the offered QoWS are conform to their descriptions. The certification we are performing is a conformance certification which represents the certification of conformity of Web services to its description including their QoWS properties claimed in the service interface.

The Web service Certifier is implemented within the broker and is responsible for certifying Web services and their provided QoWS. A certificate is sent to the Web services provider and a copy is stored in the broker's database for future use. A certificate includes information such as certificate number, certificate issue date, number of years in business, services location. If, for some reasons, a certificate cannot be issued, feedbacks are sent to the provider. This may be due to the provider's resource limitations, to its bad reputation, etc. An example of a certificate is depicted in Figure 19.

Figure 19 Example of Tri_Stat Web services certificate

Once the QoWS verification and certification are completed, the advertised QoWS classes might not meet completely the client requirements. However, clients can negotiate new classes of QoWS different from what is published in the Web services description. In this case, a QoWS negotiation process is initiated to reach an agreement between clients and providers. The next section describes our QoWS negotiation approach.

5.7 QoWS Negotiation Model

Whenever a required class of service is not published in the Web service description, involved parties can decide to negotiate a new class of service. The negotiation phase is conducted in order to reach an agreement between the concerned parties for a required level

106

of QoWS. The type of Web service and the underlying QoWS architecture play a major role in the way the negotiation is conducted. In most previous QoWS negotiation processes, such as those proposed for negotiating QoWS in multimedia applications, the first negotiation step starts with the client issuing a request that carries QoWS expectations. The provider then makes an offer, stating possible performance options related to its resources capabilities. The client can then respond to the offer, either by selecting an option and issuing it as a contract, or restarting the negotiation by formulating a modified request.

In the context of Web services, the QoWS description is known (published) in advance and described through the Web service interface description. To conduct the QoWS negotiation process between providers and clients, we have developed a QoS-oriented negotiation algorithm that defines the main steps of a bidirectional negotiation between the client and the provider (see Figure 20). The negotiation algorithm offers two options. In the first option, the client can choose from the list of QoWS classes that have been described in the WSDL document, and then, negotiate the final price with the service provider regarding its selected QoWS class. The second option allows the client to specify its QoWS requirements either by combining different available QoWS classes, or by creating a new QoWS class with new QoWS attributes and their values. The provider may then accept the new requirements as a new class of QoWS, or reject them for a specific reasons (e.g. because of resources limitation).

At the end of the negotiation process, a contract is issued by the provider and accepted by the client. The contract states the agreed on level of QoWS, the period of this provision, and the cost of the service. If the negotiation did not succeed, it will be terminated without any agreement. The negotiation algorithm is presented bellow:

```
S: {s₁, s₂, .., sₙ}                           // Provider Web services.
Si_QoSᵢ: {p₁,p₂,....,pₙ}                      // QoS properties described in the service interface.
Class_QoSi: {QoSᵢ,......,QoSₙ}               // Description of each class of QoS.
QoS_negotiation_Rules {R1,.......,Rn}    // Rules used to guide QoS negotiation and to write the
contract.
Pᵢ: {parameter name, parameter type, ...} // Description of each property

Let WSDL_Doc denotes the structure of the service interface
Let QoS_Desc denote the description of QoS attributes
Let QoS_Classes denote a set of QoS attributes with their respective values

Loop
        Either:
                Chooses from WSDLC_Doc ONE QoS_Class among a set of described QoS_Classes
                using QoS_Desc and uses them to negotiate the final price with the service provider.
        Or:
                Formulates a new QoS_Class

                Either:

                        By combining QoS attributes from existing QoS_Classes using QoS_Desc
                        and proposing this emerging class to the provider for negotiation.
                Or:
                        By creating a new QoS_Class with new QoS attributes and their related
                        values and negotiating them with the service provider.
                End
        Or:
                Rejects all the proposed QoS_Classes and terminates the negotiation process
End loop.

If negotiation is successful then

QoS_negotiation_Rules are added to the contract.
Contract is signed by both client and provider.
Contract issued by the provider.
Start QoS provision.
```

Figure 20 Client-Provider bidirectional negotiation algorithm

Once the QoWS contact is issued, the client can invoke the Web service with respect to the

negotiated class of QoWS. The level of QoWS in Web services can not be maintained

forever because of many reasons. These reasons can be the absence of control of either the

provider or client of Web services over the available resources on their environment, and

also the dynamic and continuously changing client's requirements. Therefore, the monitoring

of QoWS provisioning is required to maintain the delivered QoWS to a level accepted by the

client when there is violation of the agreed level of QoWS.

Next section will propose and describe our proposed QoWS monitoring approach for QoWS-aware Web services.

5.8 Broker-based QoWS Monitoring Model

In our work, we have considered the monitoring constraints described in (section 3.2.3.2) to monitor the QoWS of basic Web services. Therefore, we monitor the QoWS at different observation locations: at the client site, at the provider site, and/or somewhere between. However, the observation location should be chosen carefully, depending on the nature of the QoWS attribute to be measured. For example, in the case of the response time, when it is measured at the provider site, the delay and latency of the underlying network are not considered. However, when it is measured at the client site, it is affected by the delay introduced by the underlying network infrastructure as it is perceived by the client.

The monitoring process supported by the architecture presented in Figure 12 is based on a QoWS measurement technique performed by the QoWS broker entity. The QoWS broker measures QoWS attributes and compares their values against the contracted QoWS previously agreed on between the client and the provider.

The Broker component performs online monitoring of QoS-aware Web services to assure compliance with published or negotiated QoWS requirements and provide immediate QoWS user feedback. The broker can be invoked by either the client or the provider to carry out the monitoring of QoWS provided by the Web service. The Broker starts monitoring QoWS by collecting needed information from the user and the provider of Web services for the sake of observation. Then, it makes use of measurement techniques to compute QoWS that is likely delivered between two points (e.g., between a Web service and a user location). Afterwards, to measure QoWS parameters, e.g., response time, availability, processing time;

the broker needs to define in advance the measurements locations (provider or requester side), the frequency (1/T) of the measurement, and the length (Lt) of the time interval over which the QoWS parameters are measured.

The broker implements a set of functions to measure the response time, the processing time, and checks the availability of operations provided by the Web services. The broker performs periodic measurements at different points of observation as shown in the architecture (points P1, P2, and P3 in Figure 21); to gather statistics about the monitoring of QoWS. The results of the measurements are stored in the broker database. Figure 21 presents our monitoring model and the components involved in this process.

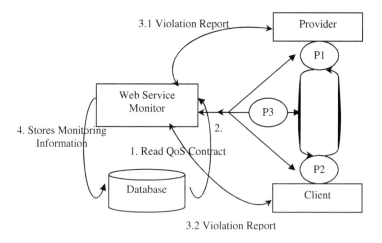

Figure 21 QoS Monitoring Model

The QoWS Monitor, a component of the broker, initiates the monitoring process and observes continuously or periodically the QoWS that is being provided. The monitoring process is based on the information described in the contract and stored in the broker database. The Web service Monitor searches this information from the database (Operation 1 in Figure 21) such as the agreed classes of QoWS that meant to be provided, the duration of invocation, the maximum number of invocations (e.g. 1000 query per minutes), and the cost per operation. Once the monitor gets the information from the database, it starts observing the exchanged messages between the client and its provider (Operation 2). The observation can be performed at different locations that are tightly related to the type of QoWS property to be observed (response time, processing time, etc.). These locations are decided by the QoWS Monitor. During the monitoring process, the QoWS monitor can detect a QoWS violation when the measured value of a QoWS property doesn't meet the agreed one. In this case, it notifies both the client and the provider about the violation, and sends to them detailed information about the occurred violation (Operation 3.1 and 3.2). Afterwards, the QoWS monitor stores information about violations in the database for future use, e.g. type of violation, name of parameters violated, time of violation, and the cause of violation (Operation 4). The stored information may be used for dynamic adaptation of QoWS and/or to generate some statistics, such as number of violation of a given parameter, the last violation of a given parameter, the mean time between two violations, time spent to recover from violations, and the most frequent cause of violations. Such statistics may be used for capacity planning, bottleneck analysis, and analysis of Web services availability.

We have implemented the components of the architecture described above. SOAP Handlers are developed and deployed at both the provider (location P1 in Figure 21) and the client (location P2 in Figure 21) sides. A SOAP handler is a special java class that intercepts a request or a response to or from a Web service before it gets to the core Web service or the client respectively, and can perform operations on it. These handlers play the role of observers that observe QoWS properties at these locations. The one deployed at location P1 is used to monitor the Web service processing time and the handler deployed at location P2 is used to monitor the Web service response time. Both handlers compute dynamically the QoWS values during different periods of time and then send continuously these values to the Web services monitor. Once received, the monitor processes and compares these values to those stored in its database. If differences are detected (e.g. QoWS value drops below a threshold values), the monitor informs both the client and provider about the QoWS violation detection and generates detailed report that describes the date and the time of violation, etc. More details about SOAP handlers and violation report are described in the implementation chapter (chapter 7).

As described in Figure 12, QoWS monitoring is achieved by the broker component. To achieve QoWS monitoring, the QoWS broker instantiates observers at the observation points (P1 and P2 in Figure 21). To measure the response time, the observer at P1 captures the time stamp when the request leaves the client and the time stamp when the response is received by the client. The QoWS broker then calculates the response time by determining the difference between the two time stamps, and stores the measured values in the broker database or writes them to a log file. A violation is detected by the QoWS broker if the measured value is above a threshold value agreed upon with the provider. Figure 22 describes the involved components in the monitoring scenarios of RT for Tri_Stat Web service.

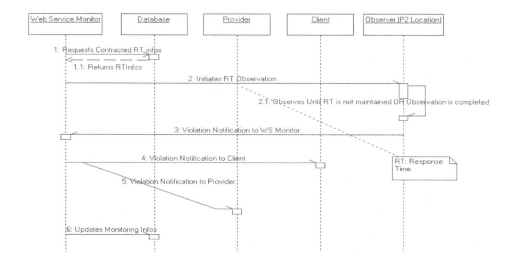

Figure 22 Scenario of RT monitoring for Tri_Stat Web service

To monitor the Web services availability, the service monitor invokes operations of the monitored Web services at different periods of time and calculates the availability as defined above (section 5.2.2.1): the percentage a Web service is up and running over the total time of observation. Using the same manner to process the RT and L, the monitor processes the computed availability values and detect if any violation by comparing these values with the contracted one.

5.9 Summary

In this chapter, we have presented a QoWS broker-based architecture (QBA-WS) for Web services. The broker component supports QoWS verification, certification, confirmation, selection, and monitoring. We described the key features of the broker that are not supported by existing approaches dealing with QoWS. The main contributions of the QBA-WS concerns (1) the design of the broker that can be invoked by interested requesters

113

when developed and published as a Web service, (2) the implementation and validation of some QoWS operations such as verification and certification, specification, publication, and discovery, (3) the integration of QoWS classes into the service interface to allow differentiated QoWS to diverse client's requirements, and (4) provide a QoWS monitoring model that observe dynamically the provision of QoWS between the clients and their providers and reports of any violated QoWS.

The applicability of the QBA-WS architecture is demonstrated in chapter 7. It provides the implementation details of architecture's components and the experiments conducted to evaluate the QoWS operations provided by the architecture.

Chapter 6

QoWS Management of Composite Web Services Architecture

6.1 Introduction

In this chapter, we develop a novel architecture, called CompQoS, for QoWS composition, verification, and monitoring of composite Web services. The QoWS composition verification is used together with the QoWS requirements in selecting Web services to participate in composing other Web services. The CompQoS architecture supports also the composition of differentiated classes of QoWS. A detailed specification of these QoWS classes through the use of ontology is provided and integrated with the basic Web services interfaces.

Extensions were added to the WSDL document of composite Web service to support classes of composite QoWS description. This new WSDL is continuously updated and published whenever changes of composite QoWS occur. A set of QoWS composition patterns is applied to achieve an analytical verification of composite QoWS. These patterns are derived from the BPEL process and are: the logic of composition (static, dynamic), the way Web services partners are invoked (synchronous or asynchronous), and the composition flow logic (pick, switch, loop, sequence, etc.).

An agent-based monitoring approach was used to monitor, validate, and enforce the aggregated QoS of a composite Web service. The QoWS monitoring process detects any QoWS violation and the concerned Web services. The architecture is demonstrated through a case study for verifying and monitoring the QoWS of a composite teleconferencing Web services in a 3G network. Different components of the architecture are developed. The network load generated by the QoWS verification and monitoring is measured, and the QoS violation detection capabilities of the architecture are discussed.

6.2 QoWS Composition Management

Web services composition is a new emerging approach of developing Web services. It consists of aggregating a set of Web services to create a more complete Web service with a wider range of functionalities. A composite Web service is also known as the final Web service. Composing Web services together leads also to the composition of QoWS offered by each Web service. QoWS composition is to leverage, aggregate and bundle the individual Web services component's QoWS properties to derive the QoWS of the composite service component [28].

Managing QoS of basic Web services is not an easy task. Managing QoS of a composite Web service is even more complex. This management will be affected by the way the QoS of basic Web services are themselves managed. For example, a higher response time of the final Web service can be due to basic Web services taking more time than expected to respond. These Web services must be identified and their response time reduced. Also, a low availability of the final Web service might be due to one ore more basic Web service that are unavailable when requested. Therefore, the QoWS management of composite Web services is tightly coupled to the management of QoWS of basic Web services. The management of composite QoWS requires the involvement of different basic Web services that offer different QoWS properties. Also, it requires a continuous sharing of management information between all managed entities: the final Web service and basic Web services. Management of QoS for composite Web services includes: QoWS verification, and QoWS monitoring.

Verification of composite QoWS properties is carried out very often prior to its publication, and then succeeded by a post-verification using a runtime monitoring. To be able to observe QoWS values of the composition, the expected QoWS values are to be provided to the component responsible for monitoring the composite QoWS. Performing appropriate QoWS monitoring will require an observation of all, or a subset of, the basic Web services. This will make the QoS monitoring of composite Web services more complex and difficult to manage.

The proposed CompQoS architecture consists of a set of components that are responsible for managing the QoWS of a composite Web service. This management includes: QoWS aggregation verification, and the continuous monitoring of this QoWS. This will identify the Web services (basic or final) that violate the delivery of a specific QoWS. The CompQoS model is proposed to meet the following objectives:

- Allow the specification of QoWS classes using an ontology that extends the Web services interfaces,

- Compute the composite QoWS values and integrate them in the WSDL document of the composite Web service,

- Verify that the composite QoWS meets its requirements in term of classes of QoWS composition and application of QoWS patterns to compute the composite QoWS.

- Maintain and update the composite QoWS specifications if the QoWS of one or more basic Web service changes (replacement, modification, or addition). Consequently, update the WSDL of the composite Web service,

- Guarantee that the global QoWS is still matching the QoWS requirements if the BPEL process is modified (e.g. composition logic is modified).

- Minimize the overhead induced by the measurement, verification, and monitoring of QoWS aggregation.

6.3 CompQoS Requirements

As stated above, QoWS properties of composite Web services are calculated using the QoWS properties description of the basic Web services. Therefore, all participating basic Web services should have a description of QoWS in their WSDL documents. Also, the BPEL document should be made available to all components of CompQoS model. A set of additional information and resources is required for QoWS composition. This concerns the QoWS composition patterns that are used to calculate the aggregated QoWS of a final Web service.

In this section, we first define how to introduce QoWS annotation including QoWS classes in WSDL document using ontology. Then, we present the QoWS composition patterns that govern the QoWS aggregation of a composite Web service and we describe them using ontology.

6.3.1 QoWS Ontology Specification

We proposed QoWS ontology to support universal QoWS specification in the service interface. Our ontology differs from other ontologies such as that presented by Maximilien et al in [74] by including, in addition to QoWS specification, the specification of different classes of QoWS for a Web service. A QoWS class describes for each QoWS property: its name, its corresponding computation unit, and its maximum possible value. This will allow diverse QoWS offers for different client requirements. In this work, we consider the following QoWS properties: response time, cost, availability, reputation, processing time, and throughput. These properties are already defined previously in chapter 5. Figure 23

represents an example of classes of QoWS ontology.

```
<?xml version="1.0" encoding="utf-8"?>
<definitions xmlns="http://schemas.xmlsoap.org/wsdl/" targetNamespace="http://... ">
.........
  <Class1>
      <QoS_Spec>
          <QoSOnto ontologyName="ResptimeOntserviceNames">
              <QoS name="response time">
                  <QoS_Value>
                      <unit>milliseconde</unit>
                      <max>5</max>
                  </QoS_Value>
              </QoS>
          </QoSOnto>
          ...
          <QoSOnto ontologyName="ThrouOntserviceNames">
              <QoS name="Throughput">
                  <QoS_Value>
                      <unit>request per second</unit>
                      <max>500</max>
                  </QoS_Value>
              </QoS>
          </QoSOnto>
      </QoS_Spec>
  </Class1>
  <Class2>
      <QoS_Spec>
          <QoSOnto ontologyName="ReputationOntserviceNames">
              <QoS name="reputation">
                  <QoS_Value>
                      <unit>rank</unit>
                      <max>3</max>
                  </QoS_Value>
              </QoS>
          </QoSOnto>
.........
      </QoS_Spec>
  </Class2>
</definitions>
```

Figure 23 WSDL document extended with classes of QoS ontology description

6.4 QoWS Composition Patterns: Formalization and XML Representation

The composite QoS properties of a final Web service depend on the QoS properties of its basic Web services and the composition patterns. The global QoS of a final Web service can be defined as a function of the set of QoS of each basic Web service. We define the QoS of a final Web service as follows:

$$CQoS_{final} = f(QoS\ ws_1, QoS\ ws_2, ..., QoS\ ws_n) \qquad (1)$$

Where $CQoS_{final}$ is the QoS of the composite Web service, and QoS ws_i, (where i=1, 2..., n) is the QoS of the basic Web service i.

Two main issues should be considered while defining QoS composition patterns of a composition process: how does the final Web service (which is a BPEL process in this chapter) invoke its partners? And how the aggregated QoWS should be calculated?

QoWS composition patterns are a set of rules that are applied to compute the aggregated QoS of a final Web service and to formulate the description of composite QoWS. These patterns are defined according to the composition logic which represents the way in which basic Web services are invoked. This invocation can be done in two different ways: synchronous or asynchronous invocations. In synchronous invocation, a final Web service invokes service partners and waits until it receives the response (blocking communication). However, in asynchronous invocation, the final Web service invokes more than one service partner at the same time in "parallel" and doesn't wait for an answer from one partner to invoke the next one (non-blocking communication). The combination among these invocation methods will differentiate the QoS of a final Web service. For each QoWS property, a dedicated pattern is executed and the QoWS property is evaluated. Table 5 shows the aggregate function for measuring the QoS attributes of a composite Web service using a set of basic Web services (Wsi) invoked in synchronous mode. Equation (1) to (6) is used to calculate the aggregated QoS of a composite Web service. Equation (1) is used to calculate the composite response time (CRT) which is the sum of all response time values of every basic Web services (Wsi). Equation (2) is used to calculate the composite cost (CC) which is the sum of all cost value of every basic Web service. Equation (3) is used to calculate the composite throughput (CTH) which is the minimum value of throughput among all throughputs of every basic Web service. Equation (4) is used to calculate the composite reputation (CR) which is the minimum value among all reputation values of all basic Web services. Equation (5) is used to calculate the composite availability (CAV) which is the product of availability values of each basic Web service. Equation (6) is used to calculate the composite processing time which is the sum of all processing time values of each basic Web service. For synchronous invocations of Web services, the aggregation of the QoWS properties presented above is presented in Table 5:

Synchronous Composition Patterns	
Composite QoWS	Aggregate equation
Response time	$CRT = \sum_{i=1}^{n} RT_{wsi}$ (1)
Cost	$CC = \sum_{i=1}^{n} C_{wsi}$ (2)
Throughput	$CTH = Min(th_1, th_2, ..., th_n)$ (3)
Reputation	$CR = Min(r_1, r_2, ..., r_n)$ (4)
Availability	$CAV = \prod_{i=1}^{n} AV_i$ (5)
Processing Time (Execution Time)	$CPT = \sum_{i=1}^{n} PT_{wsi}$ (6)

Table 5 Aggregation of numerical QoS properties

Other Asynchronous (Parallel) QoWS composition patterns were published in ([91], and [92]) and are presented in Appendix B.

We have chosen to represent the QoWS composition patterns described in Table 5 using ontology. It is described in a separate XML document which is made available to both client and provider. The patterns could be described in the BPEL document. However we have decided to separate the composition process from the QoWS composition patterns. This will avoid overloading the BPEL document and makes transparent any future modification, addition and/or upgrade of the patterns. An example of QoWS patterns ontology is described in Figure 24, with respect to what has been defined as formulas in Table 5.

```xml
<?xml version="1.0" ?>
  <Formulas>
      <SynchronousInvocation>
          <ResptimeOntserviceNames>
              <calculation>sum</calculation>
          </ResptimeOntserviceNames>

          <CostOntserviceNames>
              <calculation>sum</calculation>
          </CostOntserviceNames>

          <ThrouOntserviceNames>
              <calculation>min</calculation>
          </ThrouOntserviceNames>

          <AvailOntserviceNames>
              <calculation>prod</calculation>
          </AvailOntserviceNames>

          <ReputationOntserviceNames>
              <calculation>min</calculation>
          </ReputationOntserviceNames>
      </SynchronousInvocation >

      <AsynchronousInvocation>
      . . . . . . .
      </AsynchronousInvocation>
  </Formulas>
```

Figure 24 QoS composition patterns ontology

6.5 CompQoS Architecture Description

The architecture presented in Figure 25 is developed to support QoWS composition, QoWS verification, and QoWS monitoring of composite Web services. It consists of a set of components: the BPEL and WSDL parser, the QoWS composition manager, the QoWS monitor, and the QoWS composition patterns registry. It shows also the points of observation at which a QoWS monitor observes the communication between the client, the final Web service and different basic Web services.

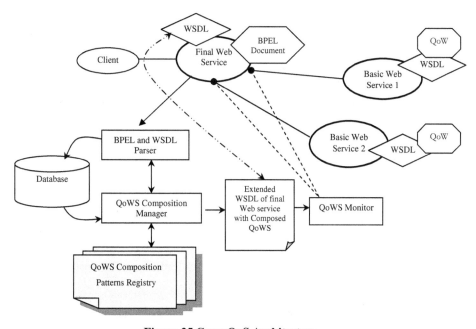

Figure 25 CompQoS Architecture

- •   Points of observation
- ----   Messages handling
- ——   Web services interactions
- —··—   File transfer
- ⟶   Components interactions

123

A description of each component and its involvement in the CompQoS architecture is presented below, in the same sequence of execution of operations achieved using components of the above architecture.

BPEL and WSDL Parser: the parser component is responsible of extracting all useful information from BPEL and WSDL documents. This information includes: reference to Web services participating in the process flow and the orchestration logic. The extracted information from the WSDL and BPEL documents will be used later on to build the sequence of invoked operations from the basic Web services. This order of invocation will be used to apply the corresponding QoWS composition pattern by the QoWS composition manager.

QoWS Composition Manager: this component is responsible for calculating the aggregated QoWS by using the corresponding QoWS composition pattern (section 6.3). Then, build a new WSDL document of the final Web service extended with the calculated composite QoWS values and their description. The QoWS composition manager updates continuously the WSDL of the composite Web service whenever changes are made on the composite QoWS values. This WSDL document is re-published whenever changed.

QoWS Composition Patterns Registry: is a registry that holds a set of QoWS composition patterns. These patterns are applied to a set of QoWS properties with main focus on the invocation logic pattern (Synchronous/Asynchronous).

QoWS Monitor: the QoWS monitor is a component that performs monitoring of QoWS composition. The QoWS monitor gets the WSDL document of the composite Web service extended with the composite QoWS description from the QoWS composition manager. The QoWS properties values contained within the WSDL document will be used after to perform conformance monitoring of QoWS composition. The main objective of monitoring the QoWS composition is to validate the QoWS aggregation of the composite Web service. The monitoring process is described in more details in chapter 7 (section 7.3).

The set of basic Web services and their QoWS description presented in Figure 25 have been verified and certified using the QoWS broker we implemented in our previous work presented in chapter 5 and published in [101]. This verification and certification consist of conducting test scenarios to verify and certify that the claimed functional and non-functional properties of a given Web service conform to its description.

In the next section, we will define the process of including the aggregated QoWS values into the original WSDL document of the composite Web service once the measured QoWS composition is valid.

6.5.1 Extending WSDL of the Composition with Composite QoWS Information

As mentioned above, QoWS values of a composite Web service is a function of QoWS values of the basic Web services. Hence, the composite QoWS properties and their values will be calculated from the WSDL of basic Web services and added to the WSDL document of a composite Web service after applying the appropriate composition patterns. The specification of the calculated composite QoWS is introduced in the WSDL document using the same ontology described above. This will take into account also the composition of classes of QoWS. The number and the type of computed composite QoWS properties in the new WSDL document of the final Web service should be the same as those described in the WSDL documents of basic Web services. Moreover, each composite class of QoWS will hold QoWS information similar to those described in the WSDL documents of basic Web services. This information concerns: QoWS properties names, threshold values, and the unit (e.g. millisecond, request/second) (Figure 23). Figure 26 describes the outline of the extended WSDL of a composite Web service with composite QoWS description. For example, a composite value of the QoWS property "availability" of Class1 is 92.1199 and composite reputation value of Class2 is 3.0 (see Table 4).

```
<?xml version="1.0" ?>
<definitions name = "Call Conference"
    targetNamespace = http:// .../CallConference.wsdl>
...
----------------------------------------------------------------
        <composedResultsClass1>
                <ResptimeOntserviceNames>8.0</ResptimeOntserviceNames>
                <AvailOntserviceNames>92.1199</AvailOntserviceNames>
                <CostOntserviceNames>1.0</CostOntserviceNames>
                <ThrouOntserviceNames>300.0</ThrouOntserviceNames>
        </composedResultsClass1>
        <composedResultsClass2>
                <ReputationOntserviceNames>3.0</ReputationOntserviceNames>
                <AvailOntserviceNames>95.0</AvailOntserviceNames>
                <CostOntserviceNames>1.4</CostOntserviceNames>
        </composedResultsClass2>
----------------------------------------------------------------
...
</definitions>
```

Figure 26 Generated WSDL of a final Web service within the composite QoS description

6.6 Summary

In this Chapter, we developed an architecture for QoWS composition, verification, and monitoring of composite Web services. The CompQoS model is driven by QoWS composition patterns and supports monitoring of QoWS composition. A detailed specification of classes of QoWS constraints through the use of ontology is provided and integrated with the basic Web services interfaces. The composition of these QoWS classes is calculated and appended into the WSDL document of the composite Web service. The QoWS composition is verified, according to a set of QoWS composition patterns, prior to the utilization of the composite Web service. Also, the composite QoWS is maintained through the monitoring of these composite QoWS. The CompQoS architecture is implemented and validated on a teleconferencing composite Web service in 3G networks.

Chapter 7
Implementation and Evaluation

7.1 Introduction

Since Web services are operating in open and heterogeneous environments, the evaluation of the components of our QoWS management framework, presented in chapter 1, is very challenging. The first step toward evaluating our approach is to implement the components and interfaces of the models we have presented in chapter 4, 5, and 6 (Lifecycles, QBA-WS, and CompQoS). The second step consists of: (1) evaluating the operations provided by the framework by using real Web services. (2) also, evaluating and measuring the interactions between the components of the framework.

The aim of this chapter is to demonstrate the feasibility and applicability of the framework proposed along this thesis. The proposed experiments we have conducted allow us to validate our design and implementation of the framework components and show that we are able to go through the process flows of the proposed QoWS management schemes (verification, certification, composition, and monitoring) for basic and composite Web services. The implementation details presented in this chapter concern the three layers of our QoWS management framework and contain the following:

(1) validation and evaluation of the conceptual model, presented in chapter 4, for both basic and composite Web services,

(2) implementation and evaluation of components of the QBA-WS architecture presented in chapter 5, and

(3) implementation and evaluation of the CompQoS architecture presented in chapter 6.

7.2 Lifecycles Evaluation

This section describes a case study of implementing and managing Web services following the development methodology we have proposed in chapter 4. The objective of this case study is to demonstrate that we are able to apply the concepts provided by the Web services lifecycle defined previously. These concepts concern mainly the implementation and the integration of QoWS management operations into the Web service lifecycle. Examples of these QoWS operations are: QoWS specification, publication, discovery, negotiation, and monitoring.

7.2.1 Case Study: A Multimedia Web Service

To show the applicability of the new lifecycle described in chapter 4, this section describes the development process of a real Web services system, which is a *Multimedia Web Service*. The MWS is a service providing the lease of videos (e.g. Films, Series, Sports shows, etc.). It allows clients to choose and load a selected video, reserve a video for future show, and negotiate the QoWS of videos with the service provider. We developed a MWS since this type of services are very sensitive to the QoWS that have to be provided to their clients. They require a high data rate due to the amount of multimedia data and the continuous nature of the video and audio. Also, clients of these MWS impose very high performance constraints on their providers. This case study describes how each development phase is completed during MWS development lifecycle, and then illustrates all the technologies involved with Web services (WSDL, SOAP, and UDDI) and how to use them in practice.

We have implemented the MWS from scratch following the implementation approach described in chapter 4, sub section 4.3.2.3. These QoWS are: quality of video, offered rate, availability, and cost. We use BEA WebLogic [115], which is a Java based development environment to develop, test, and manage this MWS. It is also deployed, and executed on WebLogic application server and published in UDDIe registry. To use our Web service, we have developed a Java client. WebLogic platform make easy the implementation process of QoWS-aware Web services. This is by providing a set of features that makes the implementation and the integration of QoWS management operations much easier for the provider of Web services.

To stream video and audio, we used Java Media Framework API (JMF) [117] which is developed by Sun Microsystems. Figure 27 depicts the participating components and the data flow during the interaction between a client and the MWS provider at runtime. The MWS provider is responsible for developing, testing, deploying, publishing, and managing the MWS before making it available to clients.

The MWS service interface describes the functional and the non-functional proprieties (QoWS) of the services being offered. A client selects, from a list of described videos, the interface description that fulfills her/his QoWS requirements (e.g. high quality video, high streaming rate, and reasonable price). Afterward, clients can negotiate the level of QoWS they are looking for via the Service Level Agreement (SLA) procedures. At the end of the SLA, an agreement is reached and a contract is signed between the MWS provider and the client. The contract states set of information about: the QoWS properties and their values, the period of the contract, and detailed information about its cost. The contract has to be respected by the provider and the client of a MWS. Once the level of QoWS is violated, a set of repercussions are applied. These consequences were clearly defined in the contract. Examples of these repercussions are: the cancellation of the contract, reimbursement of client, or the renegotiation of the QoWS contract.

To transmit audio and video streams, we have used JMF. A JMF server and client use the Real-time Transport Protocol (RTP) to support media transmission. A JMF server opens an RTP connection with a JMF client and then encodes and streams multimedia applications. JMF client receives video and audio streams, decodes them, and communicates with the Web service client who displays the streams via a media player (see Figure 28). The JMF client and the MWS client could be merged in one client application, which includes the above operations. The JMF client application is extended to be easily integrated with the MWS client application since both client applications are developed in Java. All java packages are imported in a single Java application that merges the implementation of both Web service client and JMF client.

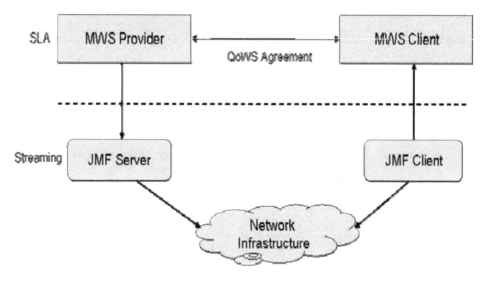

SLA: Service Level Agreement

Figure 27 MWS architecture

131

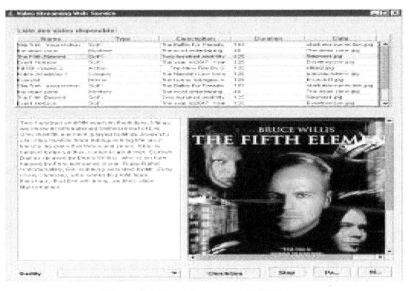

Figure 28 Client interface of MWS

7.2.2 Development Process

The first phase of this process consists of defining, analyzing, and describing the business logic of the MWS. To design the MWS, we have chosen UML as a modeling language. The latest versions of UML offer new features, which help in designing Web services with QoWS. UML offers the possibility to annotate the MWS design with a description of the non-functional properties. This helps in modeling these characteristics early in the design phase[2].

We have developed an application interface to allow the client to communicate with the server and execute a set of operations for the selection of Video, and the description of performance requirements.

---

[2] See sequence diagram of MWS presented in section 4.3.2.2

The internal logic of MWS is implemented using WebLogic Workshop source view. The implementation consists of translating the concepts modeled in the design phase in an executable form. We use the Java language to implement the MWS functionalities and we use the control points feature of WebLogic in order to connect the Multimedia Web service to its database. The latest caries information about the MWS such us: Name, Description, Duration, and Video Size.

The WSDL of the MWS comprises the definition of functional operations and a description of QoWS classes it can support (see example of Multimedia WSDL extended with classes of QoWS which is presented in chapter 4, section 4.3.2.6). The integration of classes of QoWS in the WSDL document of a MWS is not straightforward. We automated the process of QoWS specification. We developed an application interface to support the provider in specifying classes of QoWS of their Web services. The application interface allows the service provider to specify the QoWS of its Web service. For each class of QoWS the provider specifies the QoWS property name, property type, and property value. Then, the provider has to upload the WSDL document of its Web service. Once the provider presses the submit button, the specified QoWS information is used by the application to generates automatically a new and "well formed" WSDL to the provider. The generated WSDL is extended with the specified classes of QoWS description provided by the provider through the application interface (see Figure 29).

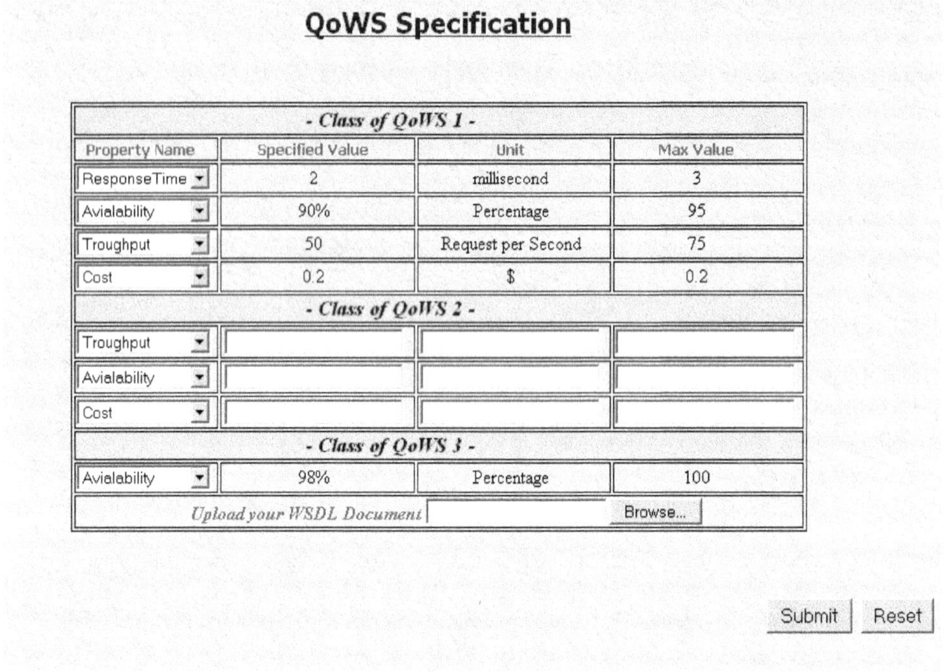

QoWS Specification

- Class of QoWS 1 -			
Property Name	Specified Value	Unit	Max Value
ResponseTime ▾	2	millisecond	3
Avialability ▾	90%	Percentage	95
Troughput ▾	50	Request per Second	75
Cost ▾	0.2	$	0.2
- Class of QoWS 2 -			
Troughput ▾			
Avialability ▾			
Cost ▾			
- Class of QoWS 3 -			
Avialability ▾	98%	Percentage	100
Upload your WSDL Document		Browse...	

Submit   Reset

Figure 29 Application support for QoWS specification

The deployment of the MWS is supported by WebLogic server, which hosts the MWS. Once the MWS is developed, described, and deployed, it needs to be published, its interface verified, and then made available to interested clients. Since the MWS implemented QoWS provision, we use the QoS-enabled UDDIe registry that supports the publication of QoWS within the WSDL document. An UDDIe client application is available for providers to publish their Web services and for clients to discover through the application interface available Web services published on the registry. The UDDIe client is a Java based application (Figure 30). We integrated the UDDIe client application with the Web services platform (WebLogic). The details of the UDDIe client application were presented before in chapter 5 (section 5.5).

134

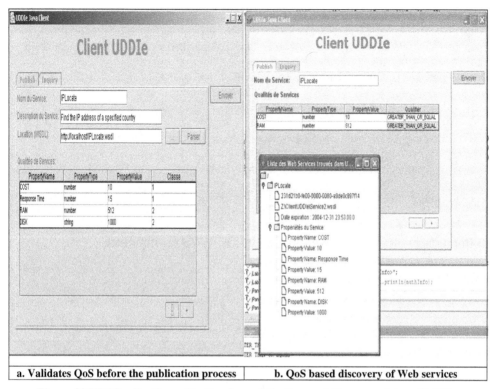

| a. Validates QoS before the publication process | b. QoS based discovery of Web services |

Figure 30 UDDIe client's application for publication and discovery driven QoWS

Testing the MWS at the implementation phase is conducted via the WebLogic Workshop that enables debugging the MWS. It makes available a number of testing features like breakpoints, and state of the service's variables. Using the WebLogic TEST_View environment we have tested our Multimedia Web service and invoked its operations from a test browser. The exchanged XML messages are displayed on the console, and all activities resulting from the interaction between a client and the Multimedia Web services are logged in files. Theses log files are used by the provider to get more details about faults generated from the interactions between the client and the service. Examples of generated fault messages are: (1) service "X" is not responding (2) input parameters mismatch.

135

The management of the MWS is provided through an administration Workshop console, which provides a deployment descriptor and allows redeployment of the MWS. It also keeps run-time statistics (number of sessions for each Web service). These statistics can be very useful for service provider to know the number of connected clients, the number of invocation during the last period, and the degree of responsiveness of their Web services.

The next section will present the implementation details of the QBA-WS architecture and the evaluation procedures we conducted to evaluate this architecture.

7.3 Implementation and Evaluation of the QBA-WS architecture

In this section, we present the implementation and the evaluation approach to assess the QBA-WS architecture presented in chapter 5. This includes the implementation and empirical evaluation of the components of the architecture mainly the QoWS verifier and certifier, and the QoWS monitor.

7.3.1 Evaluated Web Service

To demonstrate the applicability of our QBA-WS architecture, we have decided to verify, certify, and monitor a Tri_Stat Web service. This Web service provides the following functionalities:

- Computes the mean, median, variance, and the trend of sequence of numbers.

- Sorts an array of numbers passed as parameter by using three different sorting algorithms: Quick sort, Sell sort, sort by selection.

Figure 31 presents an overview of set of functionalities provided via the Tri_Sat Web service interface. The Tri_Stat describes and supports also the provision of a set of QoWS metrics as those defined in section 5.2.2.1. We decided to develop a Tri_Stat Web service instead of using the MWS developed and used in previous experiments for a couple of reasons: (1) we aim evaluating our QBA-WS on different Web services from different application domain. (2) MWS is not very appropriate for the evaluation of QoWS especially because it requires the integration of a video/audio streaming server at the provider side and also a client application at the client side (3) and it is much easier for a user to specify and validate measurable (quantifiable) QoWS using the Tri_Stat Web service.

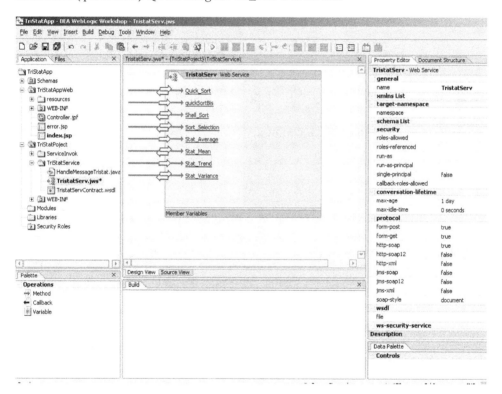

Figure 31 Tri _Stat Web service Interface

A Java application was developed to generate clients that use the Tri_Stat Web service. This application uses the multithreading API of Java to create many clients of a Web service.

Each client is a thread. The component of the QBA-WS architecture and the Tri_Stat Web service were developed using:

- WebLogic platform 8.1 with service pack 2, which includes the application server and the development environment (Workshop) [115].

- Oracle Database version 9i [118].

- UDDIe server that supports QoWS aware Web services publication and discovery [70].

The next section describes the verifier implementation and the test cases scenarios we used for evaluating the QoWS verification approach on a Tri_Stat Web service.

7.3.2 QoWS Broker: Verifier Implementation

As motivated in chapter 5, we use the verifier component of the broker to verify the functional and non-functional properties provided by a Tri_Stat Web service. We set up the QoWS verification platform, and then we configure and execute a set of QoWS verification test scenarios on a Web service. The result of these executed scenarios show how our Verifier module may be applied to verify the QoWS. In the following, we introduce the verification platform, the description of verification test cases, and the set of executed QoWS verification scenarios.

7.3.2.1 Verification Platform

Figure 32, presents the verification platform and the interactions between its components.

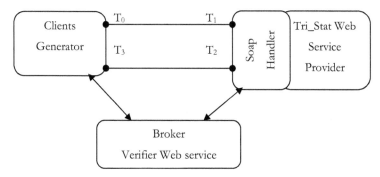

Figure 32 Verification environment

Broker Verifier. This component is designed as a Web service, and its role is to test and verify the QoS properties of a Web service (Response Time, Availability, Cost, etc.).

Client Generator. This component is a multithread Java application whose role is to generate many instances of the client that invokes the Tri_Stat Web service. It also computes the final RT value and forwards it to the Web services Verifier. This is performed by initiating a timer at the time of sending the request to the service (T_0) and by capturing the time stamp upon receiving the answer (T_3). The response time value is the difference between these two time stamps $(T_3 - T_0)$. These two times are taken locally at the client local system time. Therefore, we do not need to worry about the synchronization issue.

Soap Handler. This component is a Java class integrated with the provider service to intercept SOAP messages coming from clients. More details about the SOAP handlers and their behaviors have been presented previously in section 6.1. The handler is configured so that it can compute the processing time of each client request. This time is the difference between the time when the request arrives to the service and the time when the answer leaves the server. The processing time $(T_2 - T_1)$ is then forwarded to the Web services Verifier to compute the time spent by the message transiting in the network.

Web Service Provider: is the hosting environment where Web services are deployed and available for use by clients. The provider Web service is deployed on BEA WebLogic server.

7.3.2.2 Validation Test Cases Description

The primary goal of testing a Web service and its QoWS is to test its behavior under normal and stress conditions. These conditions are described using a performance test configuration, which identifies the configuration of the Web service under test, the configuration of the network, and the load characteristics.

We propose an approach to conduct real time test cases for three verification scenarios of RT and availability properties. Each scenario takes into consideration resource constraints that may affect the evaluation of the above QoWS attributes. The description of each scenario and its related results are illustrated below.

7.3.2.3 Tests Cases Configuration

To configure test cases for QoWS verification we need to answer the following questions: how QoWS verification test cases are defined and what are their requirements? Where and when are they executed? And what is the frequency of their execution?

We have defined verification test cases by respecting the set of constraints that have a significant influence on the evaluation of the QoWS attributes to be verified. Theses constraints include the network load, the number of clients using the Web services at the same time (scalability), the provider and the client server capacity (Memory, CPU). Concerning the requirements of these test cases, each test case needs specific requirements that can differ from one QoWS attribute to another. These requirements can be, for example, the available resources at the provider and/or the client side. The description of requirements related to each test case scenario is as follow:

The verification test cases can be executed from different locations: At the client, at the provider, and at the broker environment. Deciding from where these test cases have to be executed depends highly on the nature of the QoWS to be evaluated. For the processing time property, we have built verification test cases to be executed at the provider environment. The verification of the processing time property at the provider location excludes the round trip propagation of message to transit the network that connects the client and the provider of the service.

The time and the frequency of execution of the QoWS verification test cases is highly related to different attributes, and can differ from one QoWS property to another. These attributes include the network load, the number of connected clients at a specific time, and the resources deployed at the server side. In our experiments, we have executed the QoWS verification test cases at different days of the week, and at different time intervals. This is to verify the QoWS property of a Web service under various possible conditions that might influence the result of the evaluated QoWS property. For example, the network is less loaded during the week-end than during working days.

7.3.2.4 Execution of QoWS Verification Scenarios

Our QoWS verification approach consists of conducting experiments which involve components of QBA-WS architecture we have developed. These experiments are conducted to verify the provision of QoWS by a third party broker for a variety of clients. These clients invoke the same Web service in simultaneous way.

Our simulation model consists of a single broker, a single Web service and N concurrent clients. We measured the RT and the availability attributes using the equations below (1, 2, and 3).

(1) $RT = T_3 - T_0$ Equation (1) can be rewritten to include the network round-trip and the processing delays as:

(2) $RT = (T_1 - T_0) + (T_2 - T_1) + (T_3 - T_2)$

(3) Availability (s) = <uptime> / <total-time>

$$= <uptime> / (<upTime> + <downtime>)$$

The *uptime* is the total time the Web service has been up during the measurement period. The *downtime* is the total time the service has been down during the measurement period. And the *total-time* is the total measurement time.

Scenario 1: We generate a set of concurrent clients and we invoke the broker to calculate the RT and the availability of the Tri_Sat Web service. We have used the model described in Figure 32. We increase the number of clients until we reach the server capacity. The objective of this experiment is to check the stability of the RT while increasing the number of clients. Eventually, it will reach its limit at certain number of clients The link capacity and the available resources at the client and the provider are very limited. The results obtained from the execution of scenario 1 are illustrated in Figure 33 and Figure 34.

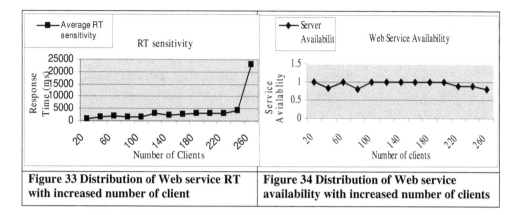

| **Figure 33 Distribution of Web service RT with increased number of client** | **Figure 34 Distribution of Web service availability with increased number of clients** |

Scenario 2: The client application, the broker, and the Tri_Stat Web service are deployed on different networks locations (LAN, Wireless) and the evaluation is carried out at different periods of the week. Also, the resources used on all involved parties (Provider, Broker, Client) are sufficient. We have used for example Pentium computers with 3.2 MHZ of CPU and 1.5 GB of memory (RAM). We first instantiate the clients, the broker, the Tri_Stat Web service at different network locations and we then measure the RT and the availability properties of the Tri_Sat Web service at different periods of the week. We have performed experiments during the week-end in a less loaded network. The experiment is to check if the RT and availability of Tri_Stat are preserved with the variation of network resources, the application server load, and the period of evaluation. The results obtained from the execution of scenario 2 are illustrated in Figure 35 and Figure 36.

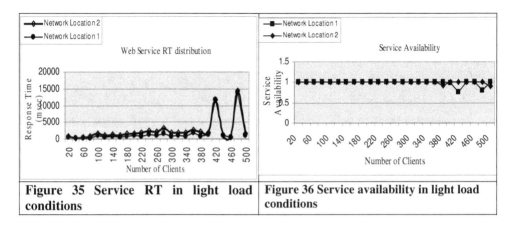

| Figure 35 Service RT in light load conditions | Figure 36 Service availability in light load conditions |

Scenario 3: We use limited resource capabilities at the client, the provider, and the broker platform (limited CPU capacity, Dial UP Connection, and limited memory size) and we try to initiate the broker to evaluate the RT and the availability of Tri_Stat Web service under these constraints. The experiments have been conducted on a Pentium PC with a 1.8 MHZ of CPU and 512 MB of RAM for the provider, the client and the broker. The results obtained from the execution of scenario 3 are illustrated in Figure 37 and Figure 38.

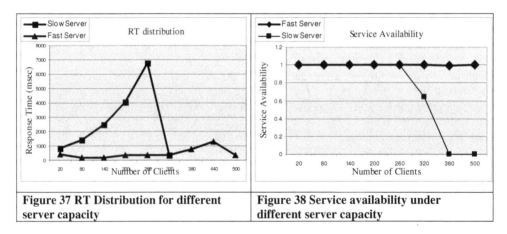

| Figure 37 RT Distribution for different server capacity | Figure 38 Service availability under different server capacity |

7.3.3 Results and Analysis of the QoWS Verification Process

The result obtained from scenario 1 and shown in Figure 33 demonstrates that the response time of Tri_Stat Web service increases linearly with the number of clients. We anticipate

144

each client to receive about $1/n$ of the server resources when n clients are active simultaneously. The Tri_Stat RT increases with the number of clients until it saturates at the maximum capacity of the server, which is 280 active clients in this experiment. Figure 34 shows that the Tri_Stat availability is fluctuating with the first generated clients. This can be explained by the time and the resource used by the Tri_Stat Web service to set up the first sessions. Afterwards, the service remains soundly available until the number of simultaneous client reaches 220 wherein it drops to 85%. The Web service becomes unavailable when the number of simultaneous clients is 280. As it is expected from this scenario, the number of clients, the network load, and the service resources capacity have a significant impact on the response time and the availability of the service.

Scenario 2 shows that when high speed network connections are used and sufficient resources are available on the server and the client's platforms, the Tri_Stat Web service can support 500 simultaneous clients from two locations (1000 clients in total). Under light load conditions (experiment is performed during the week-end) and using different network locations and significant resources at the client and the provider platforms, the Tri_Stat RT is sensibly small and stable with the increased number of clients (Figure 35). At the same time, the Tri_Stat availability is very high and stable with the increased number of connected clients (Figure 36). Afterwards, it decreases slightly at about 450 clients connected from two network location (total of 900 clients).

From scenario 3, it was expected that the RT of the Tri_Stat RT Web service is significantly larger with the slowest server and the availability is smaller compared with the fastest server (Figure 37 and Figure 38). The Web service rejects all incoming requests when it is handling more than 320 simultaneous clients from different locations. Similar behavior is observed for the availability of Tri_Sat Web service. The latest starts to be partially available at 260 active clients from each location (total of 520 clients) and becomes totally unavailable at 380 clients from each location (total of 720 clients).

Finally, the results of validation test cases show the impact of the server resources capacity, the number of connected clients, the network load on the RT and the availability of a Tri_Stat Web service. The results indicate that under light service load, the delivered QoWS to clients at different locations is the same and all clients are satisfied. When the service is overloaded, clients with higher network throughput and located on under-loaded networks have faster and more stable response time. The QoWS values computed in the above experiments when compared with the described one are still valid under the applied constraints stated above. However, the broker will exploit the results of these experiments to evaluate the RT and the availability of the Tri_Stat Web service for its providers.

Validation of the other QoWS attributes (price, and reputation) is also achieved by the broker. The service Verifier stores in its database all QoWS information published in the Web service interface. These QoWS information of each Web service are classified in the broker's database by category of application domain (e.g. online dictionary, online weather forecast) and based on the QoWS properties they offer. The verifier retrieves from the database the QoS information of Web services offering similar functionalities. After that, it analyses and evaluates the service cost and reputation of a given service according to similar Web services offering the same properties. Based on this analysis the service verifier can decide about the conformity of these QoWS to the service description. The validation of the processing time property is performed using the same architecture described in Figure 30 and is evaluated using the equation 2 stated in section 7.3.2.4.

7.3.4 Implementation of the QoWS Monitor

As presented in chapter 5, we use a monitoring model (see Figure 21) to monitor the QoWS of a basic Web service. This model employs the monitor component of the broker to monitor and observe the QoWS provision of Web services at runtime. In this section we present the implementation of components of this model including the monitor, and the SOAP handlers. Also, we present the results that stem from the execution of some scenarios for monitoring a Tri_Stat Web service.

7.3.4.1 SOAP Handlers

The Web service monitor is implemented using BEA WebLogic. Implementing the Web service monitor in BEA does not affect the monitoring process since it deals only with the exchanged SOAP messages that are independent from the adopted platform.

To measure QoWS properties, we use the SOAP handler mechanism provided by BEA platform. SOAP handlers are integrated at the provider environment if the QoWS measurement is required at the provider side. While measurement of certain QoWS attributes is required at the client side, we instrumented the client environment to support the interception of messages coming from the provider by using the same technique based on SOAP handlers. Other techniques can also be used (e.g. TCP Monitor, etc.). The problem with the TCP monitor is that it breaks a TCP connection, which introduces a delay. This delay will be induced in the measured response time.

To compute the response time and the processing time of a Web service, a SOAP handler is used to capture the date of occurrence of every event (sent or received) by the observed entity (provider and/or client). Then, the computed value is sent in a UDP Datagram to the monitor entity. A sequence number field is used to identify lost UDP datagram.

A SOAP handler is used in our architecture to measure and monitor QoWS properties of a Web service through the execution of the following operations:

- Intercepts messages arriving at or leaving the component under observation (Web service or client application).

- Initiates timers when an event happens that receives and/or sends messages.

- Forwards messages to the third party component (i.e. Broker).

- Measures QoWS attribute values; for example, measures the time consumed in processing each client request (processing time).

- Forwards the measured values of QoWS to a third party and/or writes them to a log file.

7.3.4.2 Monitoring Results

To avoid synchronization problems, computing of QoWS values is performed by the handler instead of the QoWS Monitor. Data received by the Monitor from the handlers is collected and analyzed to detect if the contracted QoWS values are being maintained. First, this data is saved into a log file generated at every monitoring period (e.g. one log file for every one hour of observation). Then, this file is parsed by the monitor component and a matching algorithm is executed to compare the computed QoWS values stated in the log file with those extracted from the QoWS contract. A report is generated to describe the monitoring results and present detailed information about any detected QoWS violations if any. This report is sent later to the concerned parties including the provider and/or the client. A copy of this report is stored into the broker database for future use. Table 6 describes the results of the sequences of monitoring scenarios executed by the QoWS monitor. The monitor observes a Tri_Stat Web service during a period of one week at a rate of 6 hours observation per day. A client application has been developed to invoke the Tri_Stat Web service from different locations.

Table 6 Monitoring report of a Tri_Stat Web service

```
************************************************************************
** MoniQoS, Web service QoS monitor                                 **
** URL: http://195.229.161.21/info.htm                              **
** Date and Time: December 12, 2005, 10:15:02 GMT                   **
************************************************************************

Monitored Web service name: Tri_Stat
Period of monitoring: 7 days (6 hours a day)
Monitored QoS: RT, Latency, and Availability

List of detected violations:
```

Response Time		Expected value: 20 ms
Tri_Stat Operations	**Date and Time of violations**	**Measured value**
quickSort()	December 3, 2005, 1:10:23 GMT	25 ms
shellSort()	December 5, 2005, 7:00:54 GMT	27 ms
statisticsOp()	December 6, 2005, 3:38:07 GMT	38 ms
Total number of violation: 3		
Latency		**Expected value: 5 ms**
Tri_Stat Operations	**Date and Time of violations**	**Measured value**
quicksortBis()	December 4, 2005, 4:19:25 GMT	11 ms
selectionSort()	December 11, 2005, 9:15:59 GMT	45 ms
Total number of violation: 2		
Availability		**Expected value: 100%**
Tri_Stat Operations	**Date and Time of violations**	**Measured value**
All sorting methods	December 6, 2005,	50%
Total number of violation: 1		

The preliminary executed scenarios presented in the table above have shown promising results. Monitoring QoWS of a Tri_Stat Web service detected a couple of QoWS violations.

Three violations of RT, two violations of latency, and one violation of availability have been detected. The information about detected violations is logged in a file. The provider and the client of Tri_Stat Web service are then notified by the QoWS Monitor on the occurred QoWS violation. This notification holds information about the QoWS violated as shown in table 6. Moreover, QoWS Monitor detected where violations of RT, latency, and availability has been occurred. This is achieved through observation of these properties in different locations (e.g. provider, and/or client, and/or underlying network location).

7.4 Implementation and Evaluation of CompQoS Architecture

In this section, we describe the implementation and the approach for evaluating our CompQoS architecture presented in chapter 6.

To show the applicability of our CompQoS architecture, and the monitoring of composite Web services, (1) we have implemented the components of the architecture mainly the QoWS Composition Manager, QoWS Composition Patterns Registry, and the WSDL/BPEL parser, (2) we have used a monitoring architecture developed by Abdelghani et al[3] and published in ([70][119]) to monitor QoWS of a composite Web service, and then

---

[3] The development of the monitoring architecture of the CompQoS model was done by A. Benharref et al., he is a PhD. fellow from Concordia University. The contribution of Mr. Abdelghani was the proposition and the implementation of the agent-based monitoring architecture, the implementation of the Call Conference composite Web service, the configuration and the implementation of observers (mobile agents), and the configuration and execution of monitoring the QoWS of the conferencing composite Web service. This work will be published in [121].

we have conducted a set of experiments to evaluate the QoWS composition and monitoring features.

7.4.1 Case Study

Monitoring the QoWS of a composite Web service is an important activity of the CompQoS architecture. Monitoring of the QoWS of a composite Web service requires the monitoring of the QoS of different basic Web services. To illustrate this, we used a composite Conferencing Web Service (CWS) developed by Abdelghani et al. ([70][119]). We first introduce the context of utilization of the CWS. Then, we present the implementation of different components of the CompQoS architecture. Moreover, we show how these components interact with each other and cooperate for the purpose of QoWS monitoring and certification. Finally, we used a mobile agent-based architecture developed by Abdelghani et al. in [119] for the QoWS monitoring of both final and basic Web services.

7.4.2 The Conferencing Web Service

The Conferencing Web service allows managers located at different locations to conduct conferences and process (printing and shipping) documents generated during each conference. The CWS is a composite Web service which makes use of the following basic Web services as illustrated in Figure 39:

- **Presence WS**: this Web service contains information on users' profiles (name, address, location, status, position, availability). It checks if an employee is a manager, since only managers are invited to participate in a conference.

- **Sensors**: this Web service detects the physical presence of users. For security reasons, managers should be physically located at their offices before joining a conference.

151

- **Call Control**: this Web service creates and manages a multiparty conference (initiates the conference, adds/removes managers, and ends the conference).

- **Printing**: at some points during the conference or later on, managers may want to print documents (e.g. meeting reports). The printing Web service is responsible for printing these documents and keeping them for shipping.

- **Shipping**: documents printed during and after a conference should be distributed among users located at different locations. The CWS informs the shipping Web service about the location of the documents to be shipped to their final destinations.

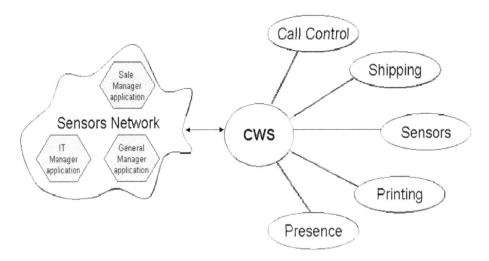

Figure 39 CWS and its basic Web services

7.4.3 CompQoS Implementation

Before the invocation of the final Web service, the composite QoWS is verified using the CompQoS architecture. The BPEL and WSDL parser of the CompQoS architecture is invoked to parse the final Web service interface. The parser is implemented using Java and SAX API for XML. The parser gets the BPEL and/or the WSDL document and instantiate the Java class "BPELParser" that uses the SAX library to parse the given document and to extract all the needed information. The QoWS Composition Manager is also implemented in Java and uses the XPath API to navigate, and find specific data in the BPEL, the WSDL, and the QoWS patterns document. The Composition Manager uses a vector to store the sequence of invocation of Web service partners. This information is be used to identify the QoWS patterns that should be applied to compute the composite QoWS. The "applyCalculation" method is used to apply the corresponding pattern to calculate the composite value of a specific QoS attribute. The "prepareExtraFields" method is used to compose classes of QoS of all basic Web services. Then, the "saveAsModifiedWSDL" method is used to build a new WSDL of the final Web service and includes the measured composite QoS values and their description. The new extended WSDL document is republished for interested clients, and is used later by the monitor.

For QoWS monitoring, we used the monitoring architecture developed by Benharref et al. ([70], and [119]) to carry out QoWS monitoring of composite Web services. This architecture offers mechanisms for online and passive observation of basic and composite Web services. Since the observation is online, misbehaviors are detected as soon as they appear. The observation architecture was initially used in ([70], [119]) to detect functional misbehaviors (faulty input/output). It has been extended by Abdelghani to support QoWS (non-functional properties). The algorithms within each observer are instrumented to allow monitoring of response time, processing time, throughput, and availability.

The observation architecture has two configurations depending on the number of observers: a Single-observer configuration to observe a simple Web service, and a multi-observer configuration for composite Web services. Since the CWS is a composite Web service, a network of observers is used to monitor its QoS and the QoS of its basic Web services. This

configuration is illustrated by Figure 40:

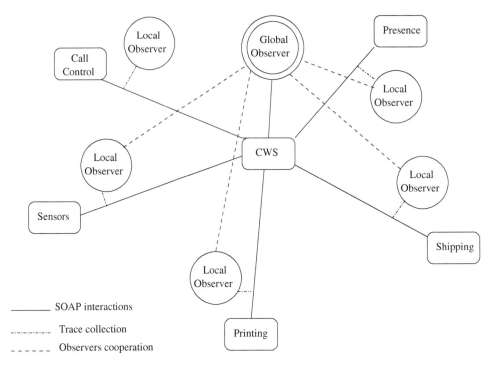

Figure 40 Monitoring the QoWS of the CWS with mobile agents

Whenever a client wants to use the CWS and monitor its provided QoWS, it invokes the

QoWS manager of the CompQoS architecture, which retrieves the BPEL and WSDL

documents of the CWS and passes them to the BPEL and WSDL parser. The parser returns

the sequence of invocation of basic Web services. According to this sequence, the manager

applies the corresponding composition pattern to compute the new set of QoWS that can be

provided by the CWS. This QoWS specification is then used to generate a new WSDL

document of the CWS.

The QoWS manager invokes the Web Service Observer (WSO) to observe the CWS. During this invocation, the new WSDL document of the CWS is provided to the WSO. This observation requires a network of mobile observers to observe all Web services (CWS and its basic Web services). As a mobile agent platform, a Jade platform is used, a free and easy tool to configure platform. For trace collection, we use the SOAP Handlers available within the BEA WebLogic. A SOAP Handler gets a copy of an incoming request before it reaches the Web service and a copy of the response before it reaches the client. This copy is then forwarded to the assigned observer. Whenever a mobile observer detects a QoWS violation, it informs the global observer which notifies the broker of this violation with full details (time of violation, violated QoS property, involved Web service(s), etc.).

7.4.4 Results and Analysis of QoWS Monitoring

The analytical verification and computation of the QoS of a composite Web service is performed based solely on the information contained in the BPEL document and the WSDL documents of the basic Web services. These are small-size documents; hence the load of retrieving them from the registry can be ignored while estimating the overall overhead.

7.4.4.1 Observed QoWS properties

In this first prototype of the CompQoS architecture, we are paying more attention to the monitoring of the response time, the processing time, the throughput, and the availability. In fact, since the points of observation are located within the provider of each Web service (composite and basic), computation of the processing time is handled at these observation points. Whenever a SOAP handler intercepts a request or its response, it appends the actual date/time, and sends it to the associated mobile observer. When the mobile observer receives a forwarded request, it reads the appended time stamp. Then, it waits for its response, which is forwarded later by the handler. The forwarded request holds also a time stamp, the date/time at which it has been generated. The processing time is then the difference between the two time stamps.

To compute the throughput of a Web service, its associated observer uses also the time stamps. The observer records all the requests that have been completely served during a certain period of execution. This process is performed during different periods of low, mean, and high load. A concise value of the throughput is the average of all the previous observed values.

For an accurate computation of the response time, we have to monitor also the propagation time between the client and the Web service. Therefore, the configuration used for the processing time and the throughput (Figure 40) does not give insights about the propagation time of a request or its response. For response time monitoring, the points of observation (the handlers) should be placed within the clients' sides. In this configuration, the Web service observer is invoked by clients themselves.

Monitoring the availability of a Web service requires explicit invocations. Clients are generated to invoke the Web service during different periods of its execution. The observers are instrumented to invoke the Web service. An observer (mobile agent) measures the availability of its dedicated Web service during a specified period of time. The measured availability value is the number of successful invocation over the total of invocations. The computed values of availability are stored in a log file.

7.4.4.2 Preliminary executed scenarios

A client application offers, through its graphical interface, the possibility to invoke any operation offered by the CWS. To illustrate some of the capabilities of the CompQoS architecture, faults have been injected to the Web services and to the network, and then we have monitored the behavior of the observers. Table 7 presents descriptions of some executed scenarios of monitoring response time, processing time, availability, and throughput of Call conference Web service. In addition, the bellow table presents the reactions of observers (both local and global) at any violation of these QoWS properties.

Table 7 Some of the executed scenarios

Target Web service	Fault description	Comments
CWS	Submit a createConference, the response is lost in the network	High response time detected by the local observer, global observer notified.
Call Control	Submit an addUsers, the Call Control Web service takes more time than expected to respond	High response time detected by the local observer, global observer notified.
Presence	Submit getUserProfile, the Presence Web service takes more time than expected to respond	High response time detected by the local observer, global observer notified.
CWS	Submit createConference, the CWS web service is not responding.	Low availability is observed at CWS web service, also High availability is detected by local observer at other basic Web, CWS is responsible.
Presence	Submit getProfile, the Presence Web service is responding as expected.	High availability detected by local observer, global observer notified.
Printing	Submit 50 printReport requests the Printing Web service is handling all requests.	High throughput is detected by local observer, global observer notified.
Call Control	Submit createConference, the Call Control web service is not responding.	Low availability is detected by local observer at the CWS web service, no availability violation detected at Call Control Web service. The problem is within the CWS web service.
Call Control	Submit createConference, the CWS web takes more time than expected to respond.	High processing time is observed by local observer, global observer notified.

157

The preliminary executed scenarios presented in the table above have shown promising results.

- All high response time misbehaviors have been detected.
- All unavailable Web services have been detected.
- All high processing time misbehaviors have been detected.
- All throughput violations have been detected.
- Most of Web services that are responsible of violating some monitored QoWS properties have been located.

7.5 Discussion of Implementations Achievements

The diversity of experiments we have conducted in this chapter range from test case studies, conducted simulation, to prototype implementation. The main goal of these experiments was to validate the features of our framework mainly the WSDLC, the QBA-WS and the CompQoS architecture.

The case study presented in section 7.2 validated the conceptual solutions provided by the WSDLC and evaluated their applicability on real Web services environment. The implementation of a Multimedia Web service case study offered the following:

- Automated the process of extending WSDL of a Multimedia Web service with classes of QoWS description. An application interface was implemented to allow the Web service provider to describe through the application interface the QoWS annotation of its Web service.
- Automated the process of QoWS discovery for client based on their QoWS requirements.
- Introduced the concept of QoWS composition patterns used to validate the composition of some QoWS of a composite Web service.

- Integrated methodologies for QoWS management operations into the Multimedia Web service development process.

The prototype implementation presented in section 7.3 evaluated the QBA-WS architecture and the QoWS management operations mainly QoWS verification, certification, and monitoring. Our primary contribution is a broker based model to achieve dynamic QoWS verification and monitoring using empirical information gathered from the involved participants (provider and client). We partially evaluate our model with a comprehensive framework for automated QoWS management operation.

In the first experiments (section 7.3.2), our simulations' results showed that using our framework, the QoWS Broker is able to accurately and dynamically verify and certify QoWS.

In the second experiments (section 7.3.4), our simulations' results showed that our framework is able to accurately and dynamically monitor and maintain the QoWS values of an evaluated Web service. Monitoring the QoWS of a Tri_Stat Web service detected a couple of violated QoWS values. Providers and clients were dynamically notified by the Monitor about the occurred QoWS violation. Moreover, the monitor was able to detect the component responsible of this violation: the provider and/or the underlying network.

In the third experiments (section 7.4), the case study implementation evaluated the applicability of our CompQoS architecture. The CompQoS provided an implementation of an ontology that extended the Web service interface with QoWS classes. It also, allowed the computation of composite QoWS and dynamically integrates them into the WSDL document of the call conference composite Web service. Using our model the service provider was able to verify that the QoWS composition requirements are fulfilled prior to the utilization of the composite Web service. In addition, composite QoWS is guaranteed using our model if the BPEL process of call conference Web service is modified.

Further experiments were conducted to evaluate the QoWS monitoring of a composite call conference Web service in 3G networks showed some good results. The simulations showed with the usage of a network of mobile observers (agents), that an optimum load is generated by the monitoring activities. Monitoring composite call conference Web service showed some violations response time, processing time, availability, and throughput of basic and/or final Web services. Also, it identifies the Web service responsible of these violations.

7.6 Requirements for Adopting our Framework

In addition to the technical aspects of components of the framework that we have described in the previous chapters, the economic aspect of the QBA-WS and CompQoS components has to be considered. This aspect is critical for its adoption by organizations. Hence, the ongoing cost associated with the adoption of the QoWS management framework has to be determined. This aspect includes the requirements in terms of software and hardware, architecture components integration, deployment and implementation. The impact of each of these requirements may differ from one organization to the other depending on the type of Web services (basic or composite) that will be deployed, integrated, or used by the organization.

7.6.1 Hardware and Software Requirements

The requirements in terms of hardware and software vary from the provider to the consumer of Web services. At the provider side, powerful computers are recommended since providers usually use clusters of servers. Each server should be at least bi-processor, with wide range memory capacity, and high performance disk storage. Each computer should have at least 5 GO of RAM, Pentium 4 (or other non Intel processor) and above, and a considerable capacity of storage. At the client side, the hardware configuration is highly dependent on the type of application platform used by the client to access Web services. In terms of software, a Web application server environment supporting Web services technologies is required. Examples of such environments are: AXIS, WebSphere from IBM, and WebLogic from BEA. Also, a Web services development platform is required to test Web services and to integrate them within the framework. Examples of such platforms are: WebLogic Workshop from BEA Systems and WebSphere studio from IBM. Also, an application server is needed to builds, deploys, composes, and manages the composition process of Web services. Example of such environment is the BPEL Process Manager from Oracle [120].

7.6.2 Integration Requirements

The operations provided by the framework have to be understood by both the clients and the providers of Web services. In addition, the broker and monitor components of the framework should be fully operational and their interfaces have to be known in advance by both providers and clients. The integration phase requires a minor configuration and adjustment of the provider's and/or the client's application when basic Web services are used. Once composite Web services are used, the integration phase requires additional integration of the components used to monitor composite Web services.

7.6.3 Monitoring Automation Requirements

The QoWS monitoring requirements are especially related to the management of the communications between the monitor component and the Web service providers and clients. In addition, it refers while monitoring composite Web service, to the communication and synchronization between all monitors deployed to monitor the set of Web services and the final Web service. Monitoring QoWS requirements are also related to the configuration and the integration of SOAP handlers at the provider and/or the client environment. These handlers are used for intercepting messages circulating between the Web services provider and clients for the sake of monitoring. Also, it is related to the configuration and the integration of software agents used to monitor the composite Web service.

7.6.4 Deployment Requirements

These requirements are mainly related to the installation of hardware and software infrastructure: setting up of the development environment, configuration of servers, testing components of the framework as well as the organization's Web services, and the deployment of the organization's Web services within the architecture. Once composite Web services are used the integration phase requires additional installation and configuration of the agent platform and the deployment of mobile agents.

7.7 Summary

In this chapter, we presented the implementation detail of our QoWS management Framework for basic and composite Web services. The implementation includes (1) developing components of the QBA-WS architecture, (2) developing components of the CompQoS architecture, (3) conducting experiments to evaluate QoWS management

162

operations provided by the Framework, (4) developing Web services (basic and composite) used to evaluate our framework, and (5) highlighting our hypotheses, our results, and states our main intellectual contributions.

It also presenting a summary of our service selection model, our framework, and its evaluation.

The implementation achieved the following objectives:

- Evaluated the applicability of our framework in managing QoWS of basic and composite Web services. Verifier, Certifier, and Monitor.

- Showed that we implemented our design and were able to go through the process flows of the proposed schemes (QoWS verification, certification, and monitoring)

- Showed empirically that the system enables a certain level of trust between service consumers and providers and a certain level of autonomy.

- Demonstrated that QoWS verification and certification is a decisive factor for Web service selection process.

- Illustrated the QoWS monitoring procedures and notifying clients about the QoWS violations that happened.

- Demonstrated that the QoWS of a composite Web services can be verified and monitored effectively.

Chapter 8

Conclusion and Future Work

8.1 Summary of Thesis

Web services are a new emerging technology for developing and/or consuming services over the internet. As these applications become omnipresent on the internet; it is obvious that the QoWS support and management of these new Web-based applications become a hot spot for the Web services community.

QoWS management has been recognized indispensable for Web services providers seeking to achieve a higher degree of competitiveness. In contrast to the QoWS management in centralized systems, the QoWS management in heterogeneous, autonomous and distributed environment presented a new set of requirements.

The objectives of our research were to automate the QoWS management of basic Web services and QoWS composition management of a composite Web service. Important concern were how to provide both clients and providers with an automated solution that provides support for QoWS management operations mainly QoWS selection, QoWS negotiation, QoWS verification, and QoWS monitoring.

In this thesis, we have proposed a framework for QoWS management of basic Web services, and QoWS composition management of a composite Web service. This framework is developed to deal with the increasing number of clients with different QoWS requirement. Our framework has been built on the basics of three layers:

The first layer defined development lifecycles for basic and composite Web services. These lifecycles integrated QoWS management operations within the SOA and their related protocols.

The second layer provided an approach to automate and support QoWS management operations for basic Web services. This solution were based on an independent Broker deployed as Web services and is in charge of supporting QoWS management functions that are: (1) verification and certification of QoWS; (2) support of Web services selection based QoWS; (3) and support of QoWS negotiation and monitoring.

The third layer provided an approach for management of QoWS composition of a composite Web service. This approach deployed several observers to monitor and enforce the QoWS composition of a composite Web service.

8.2 Thesis Contributions

The contributions of the work presented in this thesis are divided into three major contributions, namely Web services lifecycles, the QBA-WS architecture, and the CompQoS architecture. Each contribution is presented in detail below:

8.2.1 Web Services Lifecycles

We developed a model for building basic and composite Web services. We have chosen to divide the WSDLC to a set of phases to be followed during the development of Web Services. All along this decomposition, we gave more consideration to the design and implementation phases. Design phase was decomposed into sub-phases called points of concern. Each phase defines and provides a design solution to a specific feature such as QoWS management, and QoWS composition management. We have also investigated how

165

the activities of service management, deployment, and implementation can benefit from the availability of an explicit design representation that is enhanced with management capabilities. Through the implementation phase, the concepts defined in the design phase are correctly coded and service interfaces are developed.

We have developed a prototype to validate our WSDLCs model and to evaluate concepts proposed in most of the WSDLC phases.

8.2.2 QBA-WS

We developed a QoS broker-based architecture for QoS management of basic Web services. The goal of the broker is to support QoWS verification, certification, confirmation, selection, and monitoring. The main contribution is the design of a broker that can be invoked by interested requesters once developed and published as a Web service. We emphasized in this part of our work more on the verification and certification of QoWS. The salient features of the broker approach are:

1. Use of a methodological approach to measure QoWS attributes and generates test cases for the verification of QoWS.

2. Described and developed a model for QoWS monitoring based measurement techniques to dynamically observe the provision of QoWS between the clients and their providers and reports of any violation of these QoWS.

3. Illustration of the applicability of the features of the architecture with prototype implementation.

4. The QBA-WS architecture was implemented and validated through a case study of verifying QoWS of a Tri_Stat Web service. We also evaluated monitoring the QoWS of Tri_Stat Web service and the detection capabilities of the Web service Monitor.

166

The proposed architecture is a very convenient solution for QoWS management: (1) service providers do not have to design and develop their own brokers as they use one from the published brokers; (2) clients have a good support in selecting Web services using the broker services.

The adoption of the proposed architecture comes with a cost of developing a broker which should be fully operational and its interface has to be known in advance to the providers and clients. The architecture is also centralized around one single broker and might however suffer from the usual weakness of centralized architectures such as the failure of the broker (one point of failure). We strongly believe however, that the benefits from QoWS guarantees and monitoring largely overcome these limitations.

8.2.3 CompQoS

We developed CompQoS architecture for QoWS measurement, verification, and monitoring of composite Web services. The CompQoS model uses a set of QoWS composition patterns to compute the composite QoWS. The salient features of the CompQoS are:

1. A specification of QoWS constraints using ontology was described and integrated in all basic Web services interfaces.

2. Measured values of composite QoWS are validated and embedded within the WSDL document of the final Web services.

3. Support monitoring of Composed QoWS through the usage of multi-observer based mobile agents. This enforces the provision of QoWS composition by detecting violations of QoWS and by identifying the Web services from which the violations originated. The usage of mobile agents reduced the load generated from the monitoring process and eased the monitoring of composite Web services.

4. The CompQoS architecture was implemented and validated through a case study in which we observed the QoWS of a teleconferencing composed Web service in 3G networks. We evaluated also the deployment, and the overhead of trace collection introduced by the observation of QoWS composition and the detection capabilities of the different observers.

8.3 Future Work

The work presented in this thesis may be extended in several ways. Further work can be added to the three layers of the proposed framework.

First Layer:

- Extension of the Web services Lifecycles to support operations like move, update, and delete. These operations depend on the semantics of the relationships between the target service and other services (when a basic service participates in an aggregation of services).

- Inclusion of other aspects that are not considered in the WSDLC: since Web services technologies are still in their development phase, new mechanisms, and standard protocols are emerging and need to be addressed in future version of WSDLC.

- Integration of alternatives for adapting QoWS composition of a composite Web service within its lifecycle once some QoWS are violated. This can be done while taking into account feedbacks from monitoring of composite QoWS, or by dynamically replacing a faulty Web service or by scaling available resources at the provider environment.

Second layer:

- Extension of the QBA-WS architecture to support the proliferation of distributed and independent brokers from different vendors. The QoWS brokers will compete and/or cooperate collectively in delivering QoWS management for providers and clients of Web services. Work in progress to implement components of the decentralized architecture and the algorithms needed to manage the interaction and the collaboration between multiple brokers. The new additions to the architecture will improve its reliability and will enable more flexible and trustable environment with multiple participants.

- Extension of the QBA-WS architecture to support dynamic QoWS negotiation. Dynamic negotiation requires further investigation on QoWS ontology in order to define a common vocabulary for QoWS properties and their specification.

- Monitoring implementation can be enhanced to include more scenarios and involves more Web services and more partners.

Third layer:

- Support for end-to-end QoWS by implementing the mapping procedures of QoWS from the server to the network infrastructure. This will require interactions between the broker and the component responsible for guarantying QoWS at the network infrastructure. The interaction mechanism should consider the available resources, at both the service and network levels to guarantee end-to-end QoWS.

- Implementation of additional monitoring scenarios of different QoWS properties. It will also include the integration of alternatives for adapting QoWS composition when the latest is violated and taking into account feedbacks from monitoring.

169

Appendix A
QoWS Classification Model

In this appendix we describe a classification model of QoWS parameters we have proposed. The model extends the work done by S. Ran in [38] that provides an early description of these properties. We classify QoWS as a set of categories; each one describes a set of related parameters. For each QoWS parameter a brief definition is provided, its type and also its computation logic is defined (how to compute the parameter).

Some of QoWS definitions provided in the model bellow are referenced, others are not. Those that are not referenced were defined based on a deep analysis and discussion among our research group and with other people from the field.

The QoWS classification model presented bellow is divided into sub classes as follow:

❖ Performance related QoS characteristics,

❖ Runtime related QoS,

❖ Implementation related QoS,

❖ Configuration management and cost related QoS,

❖ QoS experiences Web services Users,

❖ Security related QoS characteristics, and

❖ Architectures, platform, and system related QoS Characteristics.

Appendix A-1

Performance related QoWS characteristics			
QoWS attributes (Metric)	Definition	Measurement (Computation logic)	Type
Response Time (Responsiveness)	The time a service takes to respond to various types of requests. RT is function of load intensity, which can be measured in terms of arrival rates (such as requests per second) or number of concurrent requests [39]. **OR** The guaranteed maximum (or average or minimum) time required to complete a service request [38]. QoS takes into account not only the average response time, but also the percentile (95th percentile, for example) of response time. (it include also the communication and the processing delays in servicing the client request.	For Synchronous Clients, CPRT (Client Perceived Response Time) is: $$CPRT\ (s) = \frac{\sum_{Re\,q=1}^{n} CPRT_{Re\,q}}{n}$$ $CPRT_{Req} = T(CRespr) - T(CReqs)$ (Round trip time between sending a request and receiving the response). n: number of client requests. T (CRespr): Time when Client received a response. T (CReqs): Time when Client submits a Request.	Ratio
Throughput	The rate at which a service can process requests [39]. The number of completed service requests over a time period. It is related to latency/capacity [38]. QoS measures can include the maximum throughput or a function that describes how throughput varies with load intensity.	$$T(s) = \frac{NPSR}{Period-of-Time}$$ NPSR: Number of requests processed by a service. Period: Time definition (in second, minute,) Time definition depends on the service resources abilities.	Integer
Latency	Time taken between the service requests arrives and request is being serviced [38].	$L_{Req} = T\ (PRCR) - T(PSRR)$ T (PRCR): Time when the Service Receive Client Request. T (PSSR): Time when the Service Send a Response.	Integer

Appendix A-2

Runtime related QoWS			
Web Services QoWS attributes (Metric)	**Definition**	**Measurement (Computation logic)**	**Type**
Availability	The percentage of time that the service is operating [39]. Or the probability that the service is accessible (available for use) [35]. NB: From client perspective service must be available for all time for immediate use. (This clause is clarified in the contact between Provider and Client). Service could be available but not immediately.	1. $A(s) = <up\ Time> / <totalTime>$ $= <upTime> / (<upTime> + <downtime>)$ **UpTime**: total time the system has been up during the measurement period. **DownTime**: total time the system has been down during the measurement period. **TotalTime**: the total measurement time. 2. $A(s) = T_a(s)/ø$ T_a is the total amount of time in seconds in which service **s** is available during the last ø seconds (is a constant set by an administrator of service community). The value of ø may vary depending on particular application.	Time
Reliability	**Def 1** [38]: The ability of a service to perform its required functions under stated conditions for a specified period of time. It can be measured by: Mean Time Between Failure (MTBF), Mean Time to Failure (MTF), and Mean Time To Transition (MTTT). It is closely related to availability. **Def 2** [36]: represent the degree of being capable of maintaining the service and service quality. Number of failures per mouth or year represents a measure of reliability of Web service. In another sense, reliability refers to the assured and ordered delivery for messages being sent and received by service requestors and service providers **Def 3** [32]: is the probability that a request is correctly responded within the maximum expected time frame.	From Def 3: $Q_{rel}(s) = N_c(s) / K$ $N_c(s)$: Number of times the service **s** has been successfully delivered within the maximum expected time frame, and K is the total number of invocations. Mean time between failures (MTBF) is calculated by using the following equation: From Def 1: **MTBF = (total elapsed time − sum of downtime) / number of failures** A related measurement is mean time to repair (MTTR), which is the average amount of time that it takes to bring a Web service back to full functionality after a failure.	Integer

Scalability	The capability of increasing the computing capacity of service provider's computer system and system ability to process more operations or transactions in a given period. It is related to performance. Will the system scale up to handle X transactions per second? This is closely related to throughput and performance [38].	$S(s) = \dfrac{[Mean - Capacity(s)]_D}{[Mean - Capacity(s)]_d}$ $D \gg d$ s: service d: date of the first scalability measurement. D: date of the second scalability measurement.	Ratio
Exception handling capabilities	Since it is not possible for the service designer to specify all the possible outcomes and alternatives (especially with various special cases and unanticipated possibilities), exceptions can be expected. Exception handling is how the service handles these exceptions. It can be in a brutal or a graceful way [38]. How will the service still work correctly if I give less number of parameters than it requires?	N/A (Non applicable)	Integer
Capacity	The limit of concurrent requests for guaranteed performance [53]. How many concurrent connections does the service support? Closely related to the provider software and hardware used. (Queue length, etc..).	$Capacity(s) = \dfrac{\sum_{p=1}^{N} NOPS(s)}{N}$ NOPS: Number of concurrent operation the service support in one hour. N: number of hours.	Integer
Accuracy	Defines the error rate produced by the service [38]. How many errors does the service produce over a period of time?	$Acc(s) =$ $\dfrac{Nbre - of - produced - errors}{Period}$ Period could be: Hour, Day, Month, or Year.	Ratio
Robustness/ Flexibility	It is the degree to which a service can function correctly in the presence of invalid, incomplete or conflicting inputs. Will the service still work if incomplete parameters are provided to the service request invocation?	N/A	N/A

Appendix A-3

Web Services QoWS attributes (Metric)	Definition	Measurement (Computation logic)	Type
Implementation related QoWS			
Volume	Measure of the size of a Web service (number of lines of code, number of operation provided)	Static parsing and analysis of the Web service source code.	Integer
Cohesion	Relation among operations within a same Web service.	Static parsing and analysis of the Web service source code.	Ratio
Coupling	Relation between operations of different Web services (related to Web services composition).	Static parsing and analysis of the Web service source code.	Ratio
Complexity Ratio	Average Number of operations per provided interface.	Static parsing and analysis of the Web service source code.	Ratio

Appendix A-4

Web Services QoWS attributes (Metric)	Definition	Measurement (Computation logic)	Type
Configuration management and cost related QoWS			
Regulatory	**Def 1**: It is a measure of how well the service is aligned with regulations [38]. **Def 2**: conformance with the rules, the law, compliance with standards, and the established SLA. WS use lot off standard (SOAP, UDDI, WSDL) Strict adherence to correct versions of standards (ex. SOAP 1.2 by both Service provider and requester for the proper invocation of WS [36].	N/A	N/A
Supported standard	A measure of whether the service complies with standards (e.g. industry specific standard). This can affect the portability of the service and interoperability of the service with others [38].	N/A	N/A
Stability/change cycle	A measure of the frequency of change related to the service in terms of its interfaces and/or implementation [38]. NB: We need many versions of Web services in order to measure the changes in services interface or implementation.	N/A	Ratio

Cost	It is measure of the cost involved in requesting the service [38]. What is the cost based on (per request or per volume of data?)	- Cost (s) $= \sum_{i=1}^{N} Cost(op_i)$ s: Service. op: Operation. - Cost(s) $= \sum_{i=1}^{N} Cost(VDT / op_i)$ VDT/op: Volume of Data Transfer per operation.	Integer
Completeness	A measure of the difference between the specified set of features and the implemented set of features [38]. How many of the specified features are currently available?	N/A	Ratio

Appendix A-5

QoWS experiences Web services Users			
Web Services QoWS attributes (Metric)	Definition	Measurement (Computation logic)	Type
Reputation (Client Satisfaction)	Is a measure of service trustworthiness, It depends on end user's experiences of using the service. Different user may have different opinions on the same service. The value of reputation is given by the average ranking given by to the service by end users [35].	$Q_{rep}(s) = \dfrac{\sum_{i=1}^{n} R_i}{n}$ R_i: the end user's Ranking s: the service n: number of time the service has been graded. Usually a range to rank Web services for example Amazon.com, the range is [0,5].	Integer

Appendix A-6

Security related QoWS characteristics			
Web Services QoWS attributes (Metric)	Definition	Measurement (Computation logic)	Type
Authentication	How does the service authenticate principals (users or other services) how can access service and data?	N/A	N/A
Authorization	How does the service authorize principals so that only they can access the protected services?	N/A	N/A
Confidentiality	How does the service treat the data, so that only authorized principals can access or modify the data?	N/A	N/A
Accountability	Can the supplier be hold accountable for their services?	N/A	N/A

Traceability and Auditability	Is it possible to trace the history of a service when a request was serviced? Keep tracks of served request for future usage: Accountability, verifications, performance issue, billing, etc.	N/A	N/A
Data encryption	How does the service encrypt data?	N/A	N/A
Non repudiation	A principal cannot deny requesting a service or data after the fact. How does the service provider ensure this?	N/A	N/A

Appendix A-7

Architectures, platform, and system related QoWS characteristics			
Web Services QoWS attributes (Metric)	Definition	Measurement (Computation logic)	Type
Installation, configuration and deployment	It is related to the ease of installation, configuration, and deployment. That is explained by the required steps and the provided features that help performing these operations.	N/A	N/A
Connection protocol and Message Format	It is the protocol used to bind to the Web service (Http, SOAP, WSDL), and format of the messages exchanged with the Web service (SOAP message).	N/A	N/A
Development process and Development Tools	It is related to the development process adopted (e.g. Top-Down model, waterfall model) and the development tools used (WebSphere development platform).	N/A	N/A
Monitoring & Maintaining	It is related to the monitoring features that are provided by the environment.	N/A	N/A
Security	It is related to the security features implemented by the system and provided to the Web service.	N/A	N/A
Memory utilization	It is the amount of memory consumed by the using the application.	N/A	Integer
Disk utilization	It is the amount of disk storage needed to use the Web service.	N/A	Integer
Language knowledge	It is related to the degree of knowledge of the supported language.	Beginner, Intermediate, or expert	N/A
Queues length / Capacity	It is the maximum capacity of the Web server Queues, used to handles received messages before being answered.	N/A	Integer

Appendix B
QoWS Composition Patterns

Aggregation of Numeral QoS Dimension: Mean of Execution Time, Cost and Reputation [92].

#	Pattern	Mean Execution Time	Mean Cost	Mean Reputation
Sequential Patterns				
1	Sequence	$x_a = \sum_{i=1}^{n} x_i$	$x_a = \sum_{i=1}^{n} x_i$	$x_a = min\{x_1,...,x_n\}$
2	Loop	$x_a = kx$	$x_a = kx$	$x_a = x$
Parallel Patterns				
3	XOR-XOR	$x_a = \frac{1}{n}\sum_{i=1}^{n} g_i x_i$	$x_a = \frac{1}{n}\sum_{i=1}^{n} g_i x_i$	$x_a = \frac{1}{n}\sum_{i=1}^{n} g_i x_i$
4	AND-AND	n.a.	$x_a = \sum_{i=1}^{n} x_i$	$x_a = min\{x_1,...,x_n\}$
5	AND-DISC	$x_a = \frac{1}{n}\sum_{i=1}^{n} h_i x_i$	$x_a = \sum_{i=1}^{n} x_i$	$x_a = \frac{1}{n}\sum_{i=1}^{n} h_i x_i$
6	OR-OR	n.a.	$x_a = \frac{1}{n}\sum_{i=1}^{n} h_i x_i$	$x_a = min\{x_1,...,x_n\}$
7	OR-DISC	$x_a = \frac{1}{n}\sum_{i=1}^{n} h_i x_i$	$x_a = \frac{1}{n}\sum_{i=1}^{n} h_i x_i$	$x_a = \frac{1}{n}\sum_{i=1}^{n} h_i x_i$

Bibliography

[1] COM: http://www.microsoft.com/com/default.mspx

[2] CORBA: http://www.corba.org/

[3] EJB: http://java.sun.com/products/ejb/

[4] RMI: http://java.sun.com/products/jdk/rmi/

[5] JINI: http://www.jini.org/

[6] D. Tidwell, Web Services -- The Web's next revolution, IBM Corporation. http://www6.software.ibm.com/developerworks/education/wsbasics/wsbasics-ltr.pdf

[7] BEEP: http://www.beepcore.org/

[8] IIOP: http://www.omg.org/technology/documents/formal/corba_iiop.htm

[9] MQSeries: http://www.mqseries.net/

[10] XML-RPC: http://www.xmlrpc.com/

[11] World Wide Web Consortium, "SOAP (Simple Object Access Protocol) Version 1.2", W3C Recommendation, June 2003, http://www.w3.org/TR/soap/

[12] F. Leymann: "Web Services Flow Language (WSFL 1.0)", IBM, May 2001, http://www-306.ibm.com/software/solutions/Webservices/pdf/WSFL.pdf.

[13] SOAP-DSIG (SOAP Security Extensions: Digital Signature): http://www.w3.org/TR/SOAP-dsig/

[14] BPEL4WS Version 1.1 specification, May 2003, ftp://www6.software.ibm.com/software/developer/library/ws-bpel.pdf

[15] K. Gottschalk, S. Graham, H. Kreger, and J. Snell, "Introduction to Web services architecture", IBM SYSTEMS JOURNAL, VOL 41, No 2, 2002, pp. 170-177.

[16] G. Della-Libera et al., "Web Services Security Policy (WS-SecurityPolicy)", http://www-106.ibm.com/developerworks/library/ws-secpol/

[17] World Wide Web Consortium, "Web Services Description Language 2.0", W3C working draft 3, August 2004, http://www.w3.org/tr/wsdl20

[18] http://www.roguewave.com/support/docs/leif/leif/html/soapworxug/A-2.html

[19] OASIS, "Universal Description, Discovery and Integration (UDDI) Version 3.0.2", UDDI Spec Technical Committee Draft, 2004, http://uddi.org/pubs/uddi-v3.0.2-20041019.htm

[20] CORBA Object Trader Service: http://www.omg.org/technology/documents/formal/trading_object_service.htm

[21] XLANG (Web Services for Business Process Design): http://www.gotdotnet.com/team/xml_wsspecs/xlang-c/default.htm

[22] World Wide Web Consortium, "Web Services Choreography Interface (WSCI) 1.0, W3C Note", August 2002, http://www.w3.org/TR/wsci/

[23] WS-coordination: http://www-128.ibm.com/developerworks/library/specification/ws-tx/

[24] ISO 8402, "Quality Management and Quality Assurance, International Organization for Standardization", 2000.

[25] CCITT Recommendation E.800 Quality of service and dependability vocabulary.

[26] ISO9000: http://www.iso.org/iso/en/ISOOnline.frontpage

[27] Vladimir Tosic, "Service Offerings for XML Web Services and Their Management Applications", Ph.D dissertation, Carleton University, Ottawa, Canada, 2004.

[28] M. P. Papazoglou and D. Georgakopoulos, "Service-Oriented Computing: Introduction", Communications of the ACM, Vol. 46, No. 10, pp. 25-28, October 2003.

[29] The Web Services Development Life Cycle, IBM Technical Report, 2002.

[30] K. Brennan, S. Williams, "Web Services Development Life Cycle", HP WORLD conference, White Paper, 2002.

[31] Sun Microsystems, "Web Service Life Cycle: Managing Enterprise Web Services", White paper, October 2003.

[32] J. Martin-Albo et al. "CQM: A Software Component Metric Classification Model", In Proc. of the 7th ECOOP Workshop on Quantitative Approaches in Object-Oriented Software Engineering, Darmstadt, Germany, July 2003.

[33] A. R. Gray and S.G. MacDonell, "A Comparison of Techniques for Developing Predictive Models of Software Metrics", In entrainment and Software Technology, vol. 39, pp. 425-437, 1997.

[34] N. E. Fenton, and S. L. Pfleeger, "Software Metrics A Rigorous & Practical Approach (second Edition)", International Thomson Computer Press (1997).

[35] Liangzhao et al. "Quality Driven Web Services Composition", WWW2003, May 20-24, 2003, Budapest, Hungary, ACM 1-58113-680-3/03/0005.

[36] A. Mani and A. Nagarajan, "Understanding quality of service for Web services", January 2002, IBM paper: http://www-106.ibm.com/developerworks/library/ws-quality.html

[37] Y. Li, X. DING, Y. CHEN, D. LIU, T. Li, "The Framework Supporting QoS-enabled Web Services", International Conference on Web Services, June 23-26 2003: Las Vegas, Nevada, USA.

[38] S. Ran, "A Framework for discovering Web services with Desired Quality of Services Attributes", International Conference on Web Services, June 23-26 2003: Las Vegas, Nevada, USA.

[39] Daniel A. Menascé, "QoS Issues in Web Services", IEEE Internet Computing December 2002.

[40] A. Trendowicz and Teade Punter "Quality Modeling for Software Product Lines", In Proc. of the 7th ECOOP Workshop on Quantitative Approaches in Object-Oriented Software Engineering. Darmstadt, Germany, July 2003. http://ctp.di.fct.unl.pt/QUASAR/QAOOSE2003.

[41] W. J. Salamon, D. R. Wallace, "Quality Characteristics and Metrics for reusable Software", National Institute of Standards and Technology, May 1994.

[42] B. Hailpern, P. L. Tarr, "Software Engineering for Web Services: A Focus on Separation of Concerns", IBM Research Report September 25, 2001.

[43] R. Braden, D. Clark, S. Shenker "Integrated Services in the Internet Architecture: an Overview," RFC1633, June 1994.

[44] Blake, S., Black, D., Carlson, M., Davies, E., Wang, Z., and Weiss, W., "An Architecture for Differentiated Services", December 1998, RFC 2475.

[45] E. Rosen, Viswanathan, A. Callon, R., "Multiprotocol Label Switching Architecture", April 1999.

[46] Stattenberger, G. and Braun, T., "Performance of a Bandwidth Broker for DiffServ Networks", TR, Institute of Computer Science and Applied Mathematics, University of Bern, Switzerland, 2003.

[47] A. Campbell, C. Aurrecoechea, L. Hauw: "A Review of Quality of Service Architecture," ACM Multimedia Systems journal, 1997.

[48] A. Campbell, G. Coulson, D. Hutchison, "A Quality of Service Architecture," ACM Computer Communication Review, April 1994.

[49] S. Fischer, A. Hafid, G. V. Bochmann, and H. de Meer, "Cooperative QoS Management in Multimedia Applications", IEEE International Conference on Multimedia Computing and Systems (ICMCSO97), Ottawa, Canada, June 1997.

[50] A. Benerjea, D. Ferrari, B.A. Mah, M. M Oran, D.C Verma, H. Zhang: "The Tenet Real-time Protocol Suite: Design, Implementation an experiences," IEEE/ACM Transactions on Networking, February 1996.

[51] V. Tosic and P. C. K. Hung, "Quality of Service Specification and Management for XML Web Services," in the 2005 IEEE International Conference on Web Services (ICWS'05), Orlando, Florida, USA, July 12-15, 2005.

[52] DAML-S Coalition, DAMLS-S, "Web Service Description for the Semantic Web", In Proceeding of the International Semantic Web Conference, June 2002.

[53] A. Keller and H. Ludwing, "The WSLA framework: Specifying and Monitoring Service Level Agreements for Web Services", IBM Research Report, May 2002.

[54] V. Tosic, B. Pagurek, K. Patel, "WSOL A Language for the Formal Specification of Classes of Service for Web Services", International Conference on Web Services, Las Vegas, Nevada, USA, June 2003.

[55] WS-* specifications:
http://www.Webservicesolympus.com/Webservices/WebServicesSpecifications.jsp

[56] C. Evans et al., "Web Services Reliability (WS-Reliability) Ver1.0. (2003)", draft document, http://www.oracle.com/technology/tech/Webservices/htdocs/spec/WS-ReliabilityV1.0.pdf

[57] C. Peltz, "Web Services orchestration, a review of emerging technologies, tools, and standards", Hewlett Packard, Co., 2003.

[58] G. Della-Libera et al., "Web Services Security Policy (WS-SecurityPolicy)", http://www-106.ibm.com/developerworks/library/ws-secpol/

[59] IBM Inc., "WS-T: Web Services Transaction", 2003, http://www-106.ibm.com/developerworks/library/ws-transpec/

[60] Tham, C-K, Jiang, Y. and Ko, C-C, "Monitoring QoS distribution in multimedia networks", International Journal of Network Management 2000, issue 10, p. 75-90, John Wiley and Sons.

[61] A. Campbell, G. Coulson, F. Garcia, D. Hutchison and H. Leopold, Integrated Quality of Service for Multimedia Communications, Proc. IEEE INFOCOM'93, San Francisco, USA, 1993.

[62] Y. Lu, T. F. Abdelzaher, C. Lu, G. Tao, "An Adaptive Control Framework for QoS Guarantees and its Application to Differentiated Caching Services", IWQoS, Miami Beach, Florida, 2002.

[63] Jiang, Y., Tham, C.-K. and Ko, C.-C. "A QoS Distribution Monitoring Scheme for Performance Management of Multimedia Networks", IEEE Global Telecommunication Conference. GLOBECOM, V. 1A, p. 64-68, 1999.

[64] Huard, J.-F., Inoue, I., Lazar, A. and Yamanaka, H. "Meeting QoS Guarantees by End-to-End QoS Monitoring and Adaptation", Proceedings of 5th IEEE International Symposium on High Performance Distributed Computing, 6-9 Aug. 1996 Page(s):348 – 355, 1996.

[65] Karacali, B. and Kintala, C.M. "Scalable Network Monitoring for Multimedia Applications in Enterprise Networks", Proceedings of 13th International Conference on Computer Communications and Networks, ICCCN 2004, Page(s), 329-334.

[66] Maia, J.L. and Zorzo, S.D. "Socket-Masking and SNMP: A Hybrid Approach for QoS Monitoring in Mobile Computing Environments", Proceedings of the 22nd International Conference of Computer Science Society, SCCC 2002. Chilean, 6-8 Nov. 2002, Page(s),106 - 114.

[67] Jiang, Y., Tham, C-K. and Ko C-C, "Challenges and approaches in providing QoS monitoring", International Journal of Network Management, issue 10, p. 323-334, John Wiley and Sons, 2002.

[68] Schmietendorf, A., Dumke, R., Reitz, "D.SLA management-challenges in the context of Web-service-based infrastructures", Proceedings of the IEEE International Conference on Web services, Saint Diego California July 2004, Page(s), 606 - 613.

[69] W3C Working Group, "QoS for Web Services: Requirements and Possible Approaches", Note 25 November 2003, http://www.w3c.or.kr/kr-office/TR/2003/NOTE-ws-qos-20031125/

[70] A. Benharref, R. Glitho, R. Dssouli, "Mobile Agents for Testing Web Services in Next Generation Networks", International Conference on Mobile Agents for Telecommunication Applications Montreal, Canada, 2004.

[71] A. ShaikhlAli, O. F. Rana, R. Al-Ali, D. W. Walker, "UDDIe: An Extended Registry for Web Services", Symposium on Application and the Internet Workshops SAINT 2003, January 27-31, 2003, Orlando, Florida.

[72] Sravanthi K, Shonali K, Seng W.L, "Verify: A QoS Metric for selecting Web services and providers", International conference on Web information system Engineering Workshop (WISEW 2003) Rome, Italy.

[73] W.T. Tsai, R. Paul, Z. Cao, L.Yu, A. Saimi, B. Xiao, "Verification of Web services using an enhanced UDDI server", Eighth IEEE International Workshop on Object-Oriented Real Time Dependable Systems, Guadalajara, Mexico, 2003.

[74] E.M. Maximilien and M.P. Singh, "A Framework and Ontology for Dynamic Web Services Selection", IEEE Internet Computing, 8(5), 2004, pp. 84-93.

[75] J. Zhang, "An Approach to Facilitate Reliability Testing of Web Services Components", Proceedings of IEEE 15th International Symposium on Software Reliability Engineering (ISSRE 2004), Nov. 2-5, 2004, Saint-Malo, Bretagne, France, pp. 210-218.

[76] Tsai, W. T., Chen, Y., Paul, R., Liao, N. and Huang, H., "Cooperative and Group Testing in Verification of Dynamic Composite Web Services", Proceedings of 28th

Annual International Computer Software and Applications Conference - Workshops and Fast Abstracts - (COMPSAC), Sep. 2004, 170-173.

[77] H. Chen, T. Yu, L. Kwei-Jay, "QCWS: an implementation of QoS-capable multimedia Web services", IEEE Fifth International Symposium on Multimedia Software Engineering, 2003.

[78] M. Tian, A. Gramm, T. Naumowicz, H. Ritter, J. Schiller, "A Concept for QoS Integration in Web Services", 4th International Conference on Web Information Systems Engineering, Rome, Italy, 2003.

[79] M. Tian, A. Gramm, H. Ritter, J. Schiller, "Efficient selection and monitoring of QoS-aware Web services with the WS-QoS framework", IEEE/WIC/ACM international Conference on Web Intelligence, Beijing, China, 2004.

[80] A. Padovitz, S. Krishnaswamy, and S.W. Loke, "Towards Efficient Selection of Web Services", Workshop on Web Services and Agent-based Engineering, WSABE 2003, Held in conjunction with the Second International Joint Conference on Autonomous Agents and Multi-agent Systems, AAMAS'03, Melbourne, Australia, 2003

[81] R.M. Sreenath and M.P. Singh, "Agent-based service selection", Web Semantics: Science, Services and Agents on the World Wide Web, 2004, pp. 261–279.

[82] HP Open View, http://www.managementsoftware.hp.com

[83] Parasoft, http://www.parasoft.com

[84] IBM Trivoli, http://www.trivoli.com/.

[85] OASIS, Web Services Distributed Management: Management of Web Services (WSDM-MOWS) 1.0. OASIS-Standard, 9 March 2005.
http://docs.oasis-open.org/wsdm/2004/12/wsdm-mows-1.0.pdf

[86] WS-Management, http://msdn.microsoft.com/ws/2005/02/ws-management/

[87] B. Benatallah, M. Dumas, Q. Z. heng, and A. Ngu, "Declarative Composition and Peer-to-Peer Provisioning of Dynamic Web services", In Proc. of ICDE'02, IEEE Computer society, pages 297-308, and Jose, 2002.

[88] R. Hamadi, B. Benatallah, "A Petri Net-based Model for Web services Composition", ADC 2003: 191-200.

[89] Narayanan & McIlraith, S. Narayanan, McIlraith, S.Simulation, "Verification and automated composition of Web services", In Proceedings of the World Wide Web Conference, 2002.

[90] A. Banerji, et al., "WSCL: The Web services conversation language", 2002. http://www.w3.org/TR/wscl10/

[91] Jaeger, M.C.; Rojec-Goldmann, G.; Muhl, G., "QoS Aggregation for Web Service Composition using Workflow Patterns", IEEE Enterprise Distributed Object Computing conference (EDOC), 2004.

[92] Jaeger, M.C.; Rojec-Goldmann, G.; Muhl, G., "QoS aggregation in Web service compositions", Proceedings of the IEEE International Conference on e-Technology, e-Commerce and e-Service, 29 March-1 April 2005 Page(s):181 -185.

[93] J. Cardoso, A. P. Sheth, J. A. Miller, J. Arnold, and K. J. Kochut, "Modeling quality of service for work-flows and Web service processes", Web Semantics Journal: Science, Services and Agents on the World Wide Web Journal, 1 (3):281–308, 2004.

[94] L. Zeng, B.Benatallah, A. H. H. Ngu, M. Dumas, J. Kalagnanam, and H. Chang, "QoS-Aware Middleware for Web Services Composition", IEEE transactions on Software Engineering Vol. 30, NO. 5, May 2004.

[95] Canfora, G.; Di Penta, M.; Esposito, R.; Villani, M.L.; "QoS-aware replanning of composite Web services", In Proceedings of IEEE International Conference on Web Services, ICWS 2005. 11-15 July 2005 Page(s):121 - 129 vol.1.

[96] Tao Yu; Lin, K.-J., "A broker-based framework for QoS-aware Web service composition", The 2005 IEEE International Conference on e-Technology, e-Commerce and e-Service, 2005. EEE '05. Proceedings. 29 March-1 April 2005 Page(s): 22 - 29.

[97] L. Baresi, C. Ghezzi, and S. Guinea, "Smart monitors for composed services", In Proc. 2nd International Conference on Service Oriented Computing (ICSOC'04), pages 193-202, New York, USA, November 2004. ACM.

[98] M. Adel Serhani, R. Dssouli, H. Sahraoui, A. Hafid, A. Benharref, "Toward a new Web services development life cycle ", International Multi-Conferences in Computer Science & Computer Engineering, International Symposium on Web Services and Applications, pp. 94-103, Las Vegas, Nevada, USA, June 2005.

[99] M. Adel. Serhani, R. Dssouli, A. Hafid, H. Sahraoui, "Towards an Efficient Selection and Monitoring of Web services: A QoS Broker", Submitted to the International Journal of Web services research (JWSR).

[100] M. Adel Serhani, R. Dssouli, H.Sahraoui, A. Benharref, E.Badidi, "VAQoS: Architecture for End-to-End QoS Management of Value Added Web Services", will be published in the International Journal of Intelligent Information Technologies.

[101] M. Adel Serhani, R. Dssouli, A. Hafid, H. Sahraoui, "A QoS broker based architecture for efficient Web services selection", IEEE international conference on Web services, July 2005, Volume 1, pp.113-120, Orlando Florida, USA.

[102] M. Adel Serhani, R. Dssouli, H. Sahraoui, A. Benharef, E. Badidi, "QoS Integration in Value Added Web Services", In second international conference on Innovations in Information Technology (IIT05) Dubai, U.A.E, 26-28 September 2005.

[103] M. Adel Serhani, A. Hafid, S. Houari, and A. Benharef, "QoS Broker- Based Architecture for Web Services", NOTERE, pp. 68-81, Morocco, June 2004.

[104] V. Kanodia and E. W. Knightly "Ensuring Latency Targets in Multiclass Web Servers", IEEE Transaction on Parallel and Distributed Systems, Vol.14, No. 1, January 2003.

[105] S. Hwang and N. Jung, "Dynamic scheduling of Web server cluster", In Proceedings of IEEE Ninth International Conference on Parallel and Distributed System, pp. 563-568, December 2002.

[106] E. Casalicchio and M. Colajanni, "A client-aware dispatching algorithm for Web clusters providing multiple services", In Proceedings of 10th International World Wide Web Conferrence, pp. 535-544, Hong Kong, May 2001.

[107] K. Li and S. Jamin, "A measurement-based admission controlled Web server", In Proceedings of IEEE INFOCOM, vol. 2, pp. 651-659, Telaviv, Israel, March 2000.

[108] L. Cherkasova and P. Phaal, "Session-Based Admission Control: A Mechanism for Improving Performance of Commercial Web Servers", Proc. IEEE/IFIP Int'l Workshop Quality-of-Service, June 1999.

[109] S. Schach, "Classical and Object-Oriented Software Engineering", Edition WCB/McGraw-Hill 2001.

[110] Christiansson, B., Jakobsson, L., "Component-Based Software Development Life Cycles", Proceedings of the Workshop on Emerging Issues in Computer and Systems Sciences, 29 – 30, Sept. 2000, Department of Computer and Systems Sciences, Stockholm University and the Royal Institute of Technology.

[111] B. Barn, A.W. Brown, J. Cheesman, "Methods and Tools for Component Based Development", IEEE Technology of Object-Oriented Languages, Pages 385-395, Tools 26 Proceedings, August 1998.

[112] E. Kirda, M. Jazayeri, C. Kerer, M. Schranz, "Experiences in Engineering Flexible Web Services", IEEE Multimedia, Pages 58-65, Vol.8, No.1, Jannuary 2001.

[113] J.A. Farell, H. Kreger, "Web Services Management Approaches" IBM Systems Journal, vol.41, No.2, 2002.

[114] UML Profile for Schedulability, Performance and Time version 1.0 OMG a specification document, September 2003.

[115] BEA WebLogic platform, http://www.bea.com

[116] D. Gisofli, "Web services architect: An introduction to dynamic e-business", IBM paper, 2001.

[117] Java Media Framework API (JMF) http://java.sun.com/products/java-edia/jmf/index.jsp

[118] Oracle Database http://www.oracle.com

[119] A Benharref, R Dssouli, R Glitho, M Adel Serhani, "Towards the Testing of Composed Web Services in 3rd Generation Networks", Proceeding of the 18th IFIP International Conference on Testing Communicating Systems (TestCom 2006), New York, USA, 2006.

[120] http://www.oracle.com/technology/products/ias/bpel/index.html

[121] M. Adel Serhani, R. Dssouli, A. Benharef, "CompQoS: Towards an Architecture for QoS composition and monitoring (validation) of composite web services", Accepted in the IASTED, International Conference on Web Technologies, Application, And Services "WTAS", July 2006, Calgary, Alberta, Canada.

List of my publications related to this work

Journal Papers

1. **M. Adel Serhani**, R. Dssouli, H.Sahraoui, A. Benharref, E.Badidi, "VAQoS: Architecture for End-to-End QoS Management of Value Added Web Services", accepted to the International Journal of Intelligent Information Technologies.

2. **M. Adel. Serhani**, R. Dssouli, A. Hafid, H. Sahraoui, "Towards an Efficient Selection and Monitoring of web services: A QoS Broker", accepted to the International Journal of web services research (JWSR).

Refereed Conference Publications

1. **M. Adel Serhani**, R. Dssouli, A. Benharef, "CompQoS: Towards an Architecture for QoS composition and monitoring (validation) of composite web services", Accepted in the IASTED, International Conference on Web Technologies, Application, And Services "WTAS", July 2006, Calgary, Alberta, Canada.

2. **M. Adel Serhani**, R. Dssouli, A. Hafid, H. Sahraoui, "A QoS broker based architecture for efficient web services selection", IEEE international conference on web services, July 2005, Volume 1, pp.113-120, Orlando Florida, USA.

3. **M. Adel Serhani**, R. Dssouli, H. Sahraoui, A. Hafid, A. Benharref, "Toward a new web services development life cycle ", International Multi-Conferences in Computer Science & Computer Engineering, International Symposium on Web Services and Applications, pp. 94-103, Las Vegas, Nevada, USA, June 2005.

4. **M. Adel Serhani**, R. Dssouli, H. Sahraoui, A. Benharef, E. Badidi, "QoS Integration in Value Added Web Services", In second international conference on Innovations in Information Technology (IIT05) Dubai, U.A.E, 26-28 September 2005.

5. **M. Adel Serhani**, A. Hafid, S. Houari, and A. Benharef, "QoS Broker- Based Architecture for Web Services", NOTERE, pp. 68-81, Morocco, June 2004.

6. A. Benharef, **M. Adel Serhani**, R. Dssouli, R. Glitho, "Utilisation des Agents Mobiles pour la Vérification de la Qualité de Service des Services Web" New Technologies for Distributed Systems (NOTERE'2006), ENSICA, Toulouse, France, 06-09 June 2006.

7. A. Benharref, R. Glitho, R. Dssouli, **M. Adel. Serhani,** "Towards the testing of composed web services in 3rd Generation Network", 18th IEEE/IFIP International Conference on Testing Communicating Systems (TestCom 2006), New York City, USA.

8. A. Benharref, **M. Adel. Serhani**, R. Dssouli, R. Glitho, "Une architecture Multi-Observateur pour l'Observation des Services Web composés", NOTERE, Gatineau (Quebec) Canada, 28-30 August 2005.

9. I. Taleb, A. Hafid, **M. Adel. Serhani**, "QoS-Aware Multimedia Web Services Architecture", International Conference on Web Information Systems and Technologies, May 2005, Miami, USA.